I'll Be There: My Life With the four tops

I'll Be There:
My Life With the four
tops

DUKE FAKIR

with **Kathleen McGhee-Anderson**

OMNIBUS PRESS

London / New York / Paris / Sydney / Copenhagen / Berlin / Madrid / Tokyo

Text copyright © 2022 Duke Fakir
Edition copyright © 2022 Omnibus Press
(A division of the Wise Music Group
14–15 Berners Street, London, W1T 3LJ)

Cover designed by Raissa Pardini
Picture research by the author

ISBN 978-1-913172-59-6
Signed Edition 978-1-913172-73-2

A catalogue record for this book is available from the British Library.

Designed and typeset by Evolution Design & Digital Ltd (Kent)
Printed in the Czech Republic

www.omnibuspress.com

This book is dedicated to my mother, Rubyleon, who set me on my musical path, and who I loved dearly. My grandmother, Amanda, who chose me among all her grandchildren to do hard tasks for her and instilled her marvelous work ethic in me. And lastly, my wonderful wife, Piper, who has loved me unconditionally, saved my life, and made it possible for me to enjoy the two things I treasure most, music and family. She taught me what love is really about and is the only woman I have ever truly loved.

Contents

Foreword

Most singing groups don't stay together for a lifetime, but The Four Tops did. Not until Lawrence Payton, Obie Benson, and Levi Stubbs sang their last notes did we change our line-up. Now I'm the last Top left alive to tell our story, and I've asked myself, *"Why me?"* And what kept us together for so long?

In my view, most of it was out of our hands. Something bigger was at play from the very beginning. In the middle of the twentieth century, worlds were colliding, times were changing, and people were ready for a message of love and togetherness—and they could get that from music. The Four Tops were a part of that and maybe because of who we were, a band of brothers who stuck together, known for our melodious harmonies, we were ones to sing it. My voice wasn't the one out in front but none of us wanted all the glory. We weren't the most famous group in the world, but we were famous enough.

When we first set out to make it in show business, it was a good thing we didn't know how hard it would be. In the early times of your life, everything is fresh. Every road you take is a new one and you have no idea where it's going to lead. When you look back you can see where the rubber hit the road. But at the time, we just kept going.

Along the way I felt protected by some force greater than me. Starting early in my life, several seemingly unrelated events helped navigate my direction. They occurred as visions, in dreams, and in visitations. And when the members of our group eventually met, first Levi and me, and then Obie and Lawrence, the events I envisioned came to pass.

A significant secret to our survival as well as our success was our shared belief that the sum was greater than the parts, and that time would be on our side. We knew that from the beginning, and we held fast to it. We were four totally different guys, but we had a love for the same thing, and that's basically the whole story. Four guys from Detroit who came together because of our love of music, love of entertaining, and love for each other—and we stayed together longer than any group of our era.

I believe the Great Orchestrator chose the four of us because our names represent four corners of the world. My name is Abdul Fakir, which is Muslim; Obie's name is Renaldo Benson, from the Spanish world; Levi Stubbs' name is from the Jewish world; and Lawrence Payton is as English as you can get.

Now as I go it alone, I know our story is bigger than me. It's not my story, it's God's story. There's a reason he put us together. To show, first of all, that love conquers everything. We loved singing together, living with each other, working together, and sending that love out into the world. It was always about love. In the beginning, we didn't give a shit about nothing except singing… We drove all the way across country without reverse in the car, headed toward our dreams, and there was nothing stopping us. We went full tilt toward the pinnacle of success. Not chasing the buck, chasing the dream. And we made it together.

Still, the journey was different for all of us.

❧ 1 ❧

The Road From Home

Whenever I tell my story, I begin with my father, Nazim Ali Fakir. I'm told he was born in 1900 in East India, now known as Bangladesh. He was a devout Muslim and a wonderful father.

As a young man in Bangladesh, my father had been a street singer and a maker of sitars. He eventually earned enough money to get to London, England, where he worked as a cook and chef, chasing his dream of getting to America to work in the car factories. He'd heard that any able-bodied man, no matter his skin color, could get a good job there and earn equal pay. Once he saved enough money, he booked passage on a freight boat to Windsor, Canada. Standing on the banks of the Detroit River, he looked across the forty-foot deep, three-and-a-half mile body of water and dove in. He battled the river's swiftly moving undertow to reach the Motor City, and he made it. In my life, I was to repeat a similar journey, battling seemingly insurmountable obstacles, to make it in the music business. Like my father, I overcame them. This was due in part to my unique background in both the Islamic and Christian faith, which rooted me in faith and spirituality.

My mother, Rubyleon Eckridge, was born in Sparta, Georgia, in 1914. She moved to Detroit with her parents and her six sisters and brothers in 1925 during the first Great Migration, which saw millions of African Americans move to the industrial North seeking opportunity. She met my father in Detroit as she and her younger sister, Lillar, were walking past a poolroom in the neighborhood. My father and another Indian gentleman, Mr. Uddin, caught their eye, and struck up a conversation that ended up in two marriages and thirteen children between them. Although my parents were from different parts of the world, different races, and without a common language or culture, they both believed in the American dream. Both wanted to raise a family in peace and prosperity. And both were deeply religious, musical people. They rented a house early on and had six children, three boys, Azim, Abdul, Omar, and three girls, Alladhi, Shazen, and Fatima. I was the fourth born and my mother nicknamed me "Dukie" when I was a baby, because she said I was a "little shitter." Once I started school, and heard the reaction, I quickly became "Duke." Using any nickname irritated my father because I ceased using my real name, Abdul, which represented the Muslim culture. Soon my parents' religions began to clash.

My mother was a devout Christian, who later became a minister. She played the piano and was director of the choir in the church that her father founded, Oak Grove AME. My father must have moved to the same neighborhood she lived in as a young girl because he married her in 1930 when she was sixteen. Her father helped him get a job at the Briggs Manufacturing Company, the automotive factory my grandfather worked in. The owner of the factory, Walter O. Briggs, began as a laborer in the railroad business, then worked his way up in the car industry to eventually supply auto bodies to Ford and Chrysler, as well as other companies in Europe. His story must have been quite an inspiration to my Indian immigrant father and my African American grandfather who migrated to Detroit from the South (an immigrant himself, a recent transplant from the South), both proud to be a part of America's burgeoning wartime economy.

I adored my father. When I was little, from age three until I was about five, I used to sleep with my mother. My father worked the afternoon shift and didn't come home until midnight or one in the morning. I'd go to bed, sleeping and not sleeping, waiting for him to come home. He would always bring a Coney Island hot dog home for me, which I'm crazy about to this day. I'd be waiting for him to come through the door and hung on his every word.

The North End in Detroit, which is where we lived, was a racially mixed community, a mix of Black, white, Polish, Jewish, Indian, and Italian. My father became very close to Uncle Uddin who married my mother's sister. They made their home right behind my granddaddy's church where Uncle Uddin conducted religious classes about the Islamic faith. On Sunday mornings, my father would meet me after church services in his beautiful white suit and hat to take me to study his religion and the Bengali language. I learned a few words and phrases before my mother stopped him. She wanted her children to be raised as good Christians. After that, he would show up in church screaming, "Get my kids out of there! Jesus Christ my ass!" And they would throw him out. So my parents eventually separated and divorced. I was about seven years old, and remained at home with my mom and the rest of the kids, but I remember his early influence well.

Unfortunately, my experience with Islam was short-lived. After my father lost the battle for my religious soul, I was raised in Oak Grove AME. I'm a devout Christian, but I am a product of my father's Islamic religion too. The two religions are inside of me. The Islamic faith is about peace and love, like Christianity. The main difference is that Muslims don't believe in Jesus Christ as the savior of all men. Nowadays there is division in the world and we're taught that Muslim people are very different to us, or that there is something about Muslims that we shouldn't like. But being a true Muslim is nothing like the crazy, fanatical believers you hear about now. That is not the Islam I know.

* * *

Under my mother's musical supervision, I started off singing in the baby choir, then graduated to the junior choir and eventually the senior choir, which consisted of most of my siblings and cousins, too. We all lived in the same neighborhood and our three families made up the whole junior choir. Singing in the choir wasn't an exceptional thing to do in my family, and I surely didn't have the best voice. Two of my sisters could outsing me. We all loved it though, it came with the territory, as well as helping out at home, and doing household chores since my mother worked during the day. I helped Shazen do the dishes,

The formative family youth choir. I'm second row, second from left.

the family wash and running errands. We always sang when we worked. At night, after homework and on weekends, we would play checkers, cards and Scrabble together. I didn't see as much of my older brother, Azim, since he went to live with our father when my parents split, but he kept our family's musical tradition alive, playing saxophone and eventually starting his own group. Even though music was a constant presence in our lives, I didn't realize that I had been given a musical gift until an otherworldly figure came to me while I was in a state of deep despair. She shared her vision of my future: that I was put on this earth to sing. I was just eight years old.

One day my mother singled me out during choir practice. "Duke, you have a beautiful voice," she said. "I want you to sing a solo."

I never liked singing alone. "Mama, I don't really feel like that," I told her. "I just want to sing in the choir."

I loved choir music, all the voices blending together in perfect harmony. But perhaps, among all her children's voices, she'd heard her youngest son's had a special quality to it. She persisted: "Dukie, you're going to sing this song. Your voice is too pretty not to."

She made me learn 'We Are Heavenly Father's Children' *"…and he knows just how much we can bear."* That Sunday, I stood up in my grandfather's church and looked at all the faces staring at me. My mother proudly announced that her son was going to sing a solo. I made it through the first verse and started into the chorus when I froze. I didn't feel frightened, I just couldn't sing another word. I started crying and sat down, embarrassed and humiliated. Mercifully, my mother directed the choir to pick up where I left off, and they finished singing the song.

When I got home, my mother was angry and confused, demanding to know why I'd stopped singing. I had no real explanation. All I could say was that I couldn't help it. I didn't know why I choked up. "Well, next Sunday you're going to sing that song and you going to finish it," she told me, end of subject.

That following Sunday, I was still nervous. But I didn't want to disappoint my mother, so I reassured her that I was ready.

This time I even closed my eyes so I couldn't see the people looking at me. At the same exact point in the song, I choked up again. I started sobbing, looking directly at my mother who I knew I'd let down. I dashed off the choir stand beside the pulpit where my grandfather was presiding, ran straight down the aisle, and out the front door.

Standing on the sidewalk in my little white choir robe, sniffing, the sounds of the service wafted outside. I asked myself why I couldn't finish one simple song. And then I noticed an interesting lady walk by, wearing a white headdress. She was dressed like a nurse in the church, who attended to people who fell when they got the spirit or were overcome. As she walked by, she stopped and looked at me really hard. Then her eyes seemed to take in more than just me, like something bigger was filling her vision. And she kept on looking.

"Son," she said in astonishment.

"Yes, ma'am."

"You sing, don't you?"

"I try, but that's why I'm out here. I was singing a song and I just couldn't finish." I could barely speak, holding back my tears. And before I could finish telling her what happened, she interrupted.

"Oh, my God," she said, her face lighting up, eyes glowing. "Look at all the angels around you!"

I looked around but I couldn't see anything.

"There's angels all around you, son," she said in amazement.

"What do you mean?" I kept searching the air, trying to see what she did.

She went on, half talking to me, but more absorbed in what she could see plainly and was a mystery to me.

"Do you know that the world is going to love your music?"

"My music?"

"Just listen. You're going to be singing for people everywhere."

This was even more confusing. I couldn't even get one song out. As she started walking away her last words to me were, "Always remember that love is your answer."

I watched as her flowing white robe and headdress disappeared in the distance. I wanted to follow and ask more questions. But I stayed rooted in front of the church, now even more confused by what had just happened and my earlier failure to finish the song.

Now I often think about what she said, about her prediction of my future, and the host of angels she saw surrounding me. She seemed amazed by them. But their existence has proven true or else I wouldn't be here to tell the story. All throughout my life I have felt a presence. Even as a child I knew there had to be some special forces watching over me. There is no other explanation for my protection in what have been extraordinary circumstances, or for the spiritual guidance I've been blessed with, which has come precisely at the right time and place over and over again. After my encounter with the Lady in White, the angels must have started working overtime.

A few years later, a young friend of mine, Melvin, who lived near me in the North End, tried to convince me to skip school with him. We were living on Horton Street, and there were freight trains that ran nearby on the other side of East Grand Boulevard.

"Duke, come on, let's skip school tomorrow and jump on them trains," Melvin said excitedly.

The idea of hopping a train and riding on top of the world was thrilling to me. "Ooh," I said, "that sounds exciting."

But I had never skipped school before, and it made me uneasy. As I was getting ready to leave the house the next morning, something deep inside me said, "Boy, you go to school." While I contemplated what to do, as plain as day the voice inside me said, "GO TO SCHOOL, BOY!" I had no idea where that voice came from or whose it was, but it was strong enough to make me take a step back.

When Melvin met me on the corner, ready to embark on our adventure, I apologized, "Naw, man, I better go to school." I lived only a half block away from Palmer Elementary. "It's too close to home. Maybe next time." I wasn't sure if he'd go without me, but I went to school and put it out of my mind.

Later, as I walked home, I saw some kind of commotion up ahead. A large crowd was gathered with fire engines, police cars, and an ambulance. Someone spotted me and waved me over, saying, "Duke, you know your little friend Melvin? He fell off a train and got ground up. Crushed so bad they could barely recognize his body." I was so shocked and hurt I cried like a baby. That was the first time I seriously considered my encounter with the Lady in White, and what she'd said to me about the angels. That's when I started believing that I was protected in some kind of way, and I started listening to those inner voices.

* * *

My maternal grandmother, Amanda, was the other person who singled me out when I was a child and made me feel special. She instilled a strong work ethic in me. From the time I was big enough to pick up a mop or broom, every Saturday she paid me to clean her floors. She made me go to the shed behind the house and cut up wood for her pot-bellied stove, or run to the store to buy groceries. She picked me even though I had two brothers and three sisters, and she had other grandchildren, all of my cousins on my mother's side. They all lived closer to her, across the street and around the corner, but she picked me to run her errands although I lived a couple blocks away. Maybe because I was friendly; I was a nice kid and never complained. My mother boasted that she never had a problem out of me. And from early photos of me in the choir, I seemed to have a sweet angelic face. Whatever it was, my grandmother's love and her singling me out helped build my confidence, which served me well, especially when I faced challenges and setbacks later on in life.

My mother and grandmother's early lessons in hard work proved useful at school too. During World War II, patriotism was in full swing and I was as patriotic as they got. Twice a year, week-long paper drives were conducted to collect old newspapers and magazines to recycle. Paper was needed to pack weapons and equipment to ship overseas. I led the drive at my elementary school and was proud of the stacks and stacks of paper piled high in the schoolyard. I was even prouder when our school won an award for our contribution to the war effort.

My enthusiasm for school was so great I'd arrive ten minutes early just so I could be the first one there. One day the principal noticed me outside waiting.

"Abdul, why are you out here so early every morning?"

I didn't really have much of an answer. I just smiled happily and said, "I'm just ready to go to school."

'Tell you what," she said, impressed, "I'm going to make you the flag boy. You can raise up the flag every day." Once again, I felt like I was singled out, that I was special. I knew that my father loved the United States and treasured being a recent citizen. Now his son was in charge of raising the country's flag.

I was a proud American kid who enjoyed school, my childhood, and most of all my home. Our house was full of love. I knew my mom worked really hard to take care of us, so I tried hard not to give her any trouble.

After my initial aborted attempt at singing a solo, I began to really love music and was disappointed when the director of the school choir informed me that my voice wasn't good enough to sing that year. Once again, I was devastated because of something to do with music, and I ran home to tell my mother. She just smiled and explained that my voice was changing. She reassured me that by the next year it would be alright. She was right. After my adolescence passed and my voice changed, I joined the choir again. At the time, neither she nor I had any idea just how much music would mean to me. Although, when a doctor recommended that my tonsils be removed after I contracted tonsillitis, I flatly refused. I don't know why. I just felt like it might change my vocal quality somehow. Something was telling me no, and I said to my mom, "Please, don't let them do that, Mom." She listened to me.

* * *

At Pershing High School, I began competing in sports, and I went out for the basketball, football, and track teams. I began to concentrate more on athletics than schoolwork, which I took for granted because I was pretty smart. I got good grades in all my classes, especially chemistry. As a kid I got great gifts for my birthday and Christmas (which were a day apart) and one year I was given a chemistry set, which I loved. The subject just came to me naturally. I easily picked up on the different signs, equations, and formulas. Whatever the teacher put on the board, I could understand.

Because I wanted to go to college, I took the college preparatory class in chemistry. In the third week, I lost my book. At this point my family was very poor. My mother had remarried and my stepfather injured his back on the job at the American Cinderblock Company and he couldn't work without help. I tried to help him before I went to school, starting at four o'clock each morning. I would then run to my classes and go straight back afterwards, at the end of his shift. Our family was struggling to make ends meet, and I didn't want to tell my mom

I'd lost my book or ask her to pay for a new one. So I decided I would have to do as well as I could without a book. I never even told my teacher. I don't know why, but I totally enjoyed the challenge. Later, I relished the idea that I got through the whole class without a book. I didn't get an A, but I was proud I managed to get a B. More than anything, this was further affirmation that I could overcome any challenge if I just stuck to the task and worked hard enough.

While I was at Pershing High my first year, I really started missing my dad. I told him so, and he said, "Come stay with me for a little while." So I moved in to his place, and we actually slept in the same bed. We had some good conversations. He would talk to me about the Muslims here in America. He did not want me to get affiliated with them. In fact, I think he even mentioned Louis Farrakhan as a young man, because he was just starting to preach about Islamic stuff in Detroit. I listened to everything my dad said, and I really enjoyed being with him. The only challenge was that in 1953 there was a major bus strike in the city. He lived at Vernor Highway and John R., which was seven miles away from Pershing High School. I walked down Woodward seven miles every morning and then walked east another good half a mile, and it didn't bother me at all. I wasn't thinking about the journey; I had things on my mind as I walked, hoping and dreaming. I still got to school early, because to me being on time is late. After school I walked all the way back. I did that for a whole week and I didn't mind one bit. Being able to spend time with my dad was all that mattered.

Back then the things that motivated me were family, sports, school, and music, in equal measure. But music began creeping in slowly and taking over. How could it not? Everyone in Detroit was caught up in the rhythm. Music was in the air; it was on the street corner, in your church, blaring from passing cars, drifting out of houses, in every restaurant, bar, dry cleaners, bowling alley or skating rink, on people's lips, crackling on transistor radios. Even the assembly lines in the automotive plants hummed in unison. Cash registers jingled and jangled on Fridays louder than any day of the week. And on Sunday mornings the joyful cries of "amen" and "hallelujah" rung out in every Black neighborhood, from the riverfront all the way to Eight Mile Road, where the city spilled into the suburbs and white folks were nodding to the sounds of the city too. There was a doo-wop group on every corner and talent shows nearly every week of the year. Growing up in Detroit in the 40s, 50s and 60s music was a part of your DNA. It was as natural to us as breathing.

Everybody knew the names of all the popular artists and musicians who either hailed from Detroit or hung out there so long it was like home. Jackie Wilson, Della Reese, Nat King Cole, Billy Eckstine, Sammy Davis Jr., Louis Armstrong, Ella Fitzgerald, Count Basie: they predominated the music scene. Of all the acts, I gravitated towards those playing standards and popular music—songs from the Great American Song Book—like Eckstine and Sarah Vaughan.

When a Black artist played in Detroit, they were often booked at the Paradise Theater on Woodward Avenue, a concert hall built in 1919 for the Detroit Symphony orchestra that became an important venue for Black rhythm and blues and jazz artists in the 40s and early 50s. It looked like a majestic palace or temple, and it boasted perfect acoustics.

One night, as a young kid of thirteen years old, I made my way to the Paradise to hear the line-up. Lucky Millinder's Big Band was playing and they announced they had a young guest singing with them, Levi Stubbs, who was definitely going to be a star. He was eleven years old at the time and Jackie Wilson's first cousin. When he started singing, I was blown away. "*Shit, this boy can really sing!*" He left an indelible impression on me. I made a point to go meet him after the show, not knowing that in a couple of years our paths would cross again, and we would become great friends.

There was so much beautiful musical talent coming out of Detroit's ghetto in that era, it was like a blooming garden. I went out for the school choir when I first started at Northern High, where I went for my first semester of high school, before I transferred to Pershing. Their choir was really good, and I was excited to join. At the start, the choir teacher tested all the voices and rated us in terms of our musical knowledge and vocal ability. In the tenor section were four first tenors, just like musicians in an orchestra section, then four second tenors, etc., up to five. I was the number two tenor in the first section. The number one tenor was a good-looking, confident guy who could read music and had perfect pitch. I was a bit intimidated by him since I couldn't read music that well. We were learning Handel's 'Messiah' for Christmas and I was stumbling through, observing him singing the tenor part so beautifully that it seemed effortless.

"Who is this sucker?" I said to myself, a bit jealous, and totally in awe.

But at the same time I was learning from him. He was encouraging: "You catching up, you catching up..." he said. "You'll get it."

Years later as I moved up in my singing career, I realized that that guy in the Northern High School choir with me was George Shirley, the first Black tenor to sing a leading role in the Metropolitan Opera Company. When I passed through New York in the 60s, I'd see his name up on the Met Opera House marquee as lead tenor. I found a way to get in touch with him and we met up backstage. George recognized me and said laughingly, "Oh, you were that motherfucker who was stumbling over those notes. You're one of the Tops! You're doing really good for yourself." I was happy to let him know I wasn't a total loser. It was nice to think back to where we both started and where we came from. That we were the number one and number two tenors in the first tenor section of an all-Black high school. Who would have thought that two young Black guys from the Detroit ghetto could go so far?

I met up with Levi again after my family moved from the North End to Conant Gardens, which is when I transferred to Pershing High, where Levi was also a student. Although Levi didn't compete, when the track, football, and basketball teams went to games, he would ride on the bus with us and lead everybody in singing, like a pep rally. He got the coaches to sing, as well as the members of the team, and that's when we started to get close. But it wasn't until we survived a horrible gang fight that our deep friendship began.

Before moving from the North End, I had joined a gang, the Shakers. I joined because my big brother, Azim, was a member. I was still a little young, they called me "a little Shaker," and I wasn't fully aware of what being a gang member meant. When my brother left for the Air Force and when we moved to the new neighborhood, I became a member of the local gang there, the Gigolos. As a Gigolo, I never joined in with the fighting. I was a good guy and managed somehow to ease my way out of fights and spend all my time playing sports. But when Azim returned home from the military, someone in the Gigolos got wind that we used to be Shakers, their arch enemies.

One night, leaving a party with Azim, Levi, and a few of our friends, thirty or forty of the Gigolos jumped me and my brother. They heard we'd been members of their rival gang and they were outraged. They started kicking my butt right behind Pershing High School. We were getting beaten pretty badly, but there were so many of them against Azim and me, it was hard for Levi to help us. Everyone was fist-fighting until one guy threw me up against a car and broke a Coke bottle in full gang-rage mode. He was about to stab me in the face when Levi grabbed his arm, pleading, "Nah nah, man. Please, don't do that. Just fight him, beat him up. But don't do that."

Levi was the kind of guy everybody liked. He stood apart from everything, always on the fence, keeping his distance from violence and gang wars. But he stopped this guy from busting me in the face with a broken bottle. The dude threw it away, but he continued kicking my ass. By the time they finished, I was on the ground, scarred up, barely able to move, crawling on my hands and knees. My brother was hurt pretty badly too, and he wanted revenge. "I'm going back to North End and getting some Shakers. We're going to get these guys," he said, hauling me to my feet.

I wasn't opposed to it, but I was beaten up so badly that he took me home to lick my wounds while he drove over to the North End. When he came back with the Shakers, he picked me up, and we all headed over to Joanne's restaurant where we knew the Gigolos were hanging out. Of all people, Levi was the first guy to walk out of Joanne's. One of the Shakers, a real tough guy, "Two Knives Penniman," whipped out his two knives ready to stab Levi, when this time I stepped in and yelled, "Naw don't, don't do that, that's my guy. The guys we want are in the restaurant," pointing to the door of Joanne's.

As they ran inside, I grabbed Levi and jumped back in the car, freaked out, still quaking from the earlier fight. Azim knew I was too injured to take part in another brawl. My face was bleeding, I had cuts on my knees (scars I still have to this day), and my pants were all torn up. My brother told me to go home, promising me that he'd finish it off.

Levi and I left the scene of the big gang fight and ran back to my house, which was just a block or two away. From that day on, Levi stayed with me and my family. His family's apartment in the project was too crowded and my house had a basement where we could spread out and make our own living quarters.

We lived there like siblings until after graduation. At first it had been about the singing, but that night we saved each other's lives. The forces that brought us together seemed inevitable. And once again, angels seemed to be looking after me. Even now I shudder when I think of how close I have come to disaster throughout my life. I somehow avoided failure, death, disfigurement, addiction, and even ending the life of someone I dearly loved.

Azim had given me a 45 pistol to protect myself in case something like the big gang fight jumped off again. One day I was in the basement washing clothes with my oldest sister, Shazen, and I pulled out my new gun, showing off. I had taken all the bullets out. "Look, Shi," I said. "Look what Az gave me." I pointed it at her head and pulled the trigger. CLICK; it didn't go off.

She reacted, pissed. "Don't do that, Dukie, stop! It might have a bullet in there."

"Ain't no bullet in there," I said playfully, pointing it above me. I pulled the trigger again. BAM! A bullet blasted straight through the ceiling. It went clear through the house out the roof. We were shocked.

"Thank God, that bullet didn't hit me," Shi said, as we both stood there shaking. "You almost killed me." I almost cried, thinking about how close I came to blowing my dear sister's head off. I'm still scared. The only sense I can make of it not happening is that there's a reason for me being here, a job I had to do; something bigger than me, saving me for something.

Even though I knew I was lucky and sensed that a higher power was looking out for me, it still didn't point me in the direction of what I should do with my life. Plenty of guys in my neighborhood gravitated to the street, joining gangs and hustling. But in 1954, as my senior year was ending, I wanted to go to college. I knew I would need a scholarship, so I approached Mr. Morris, who had been my basketball coach during my one semester at Northern. (The white coach at Pershing High came up with no scholarship offers.) Mr. Morris had admired my playing when I was on his team. With his help I got an athletic scholarship to Central State in Ohio, a historically Black college across the street from Wilberforce University. He encouraged me to go, but he was frank about the financial challenges.

"It's a very small scholarship," he said. "You're going to need some extra money because this doesn't cover everything. But they'll be looking for you in September."

"Coach, if it covers anything, I'm happy," I said, determined to find a way.

With the help of my mom, I set out to apply for city and state jobs to earn the extra money, but another opportunity quickly presented itself. Levi was still living with me and on the streets he heard about a guy in Toledo, Welton E. Barnett, who was trying to put together a singing group to perform at the Wolhurst Country Club in Littleton, Colorado. It seemed like a good chance to make some money, and we felt we could sing as well as anybody. So we got someone to drive us to Toledo to talk to Barnett, a very intelligent guy who published a small Black newspaper. Barnett was interested in us if we agreed to back up his lead singer, some guy who had just gotten out of prison and may have been his boyfriend. This was okay with us, especially since the money was good, a couple hundred bucks each for a one-week engagement. We went back to Detroit and recruited another singer, a guy named John, who worked with Jackie Wilson and had a great voice. The engagement was close to New Year's and, coupled with the holiday spirit, our expectations were high. This was our first professional job, and we were ready and excited.

Barnett paid for our bus fare to Denver, and we checked into the YMCA, anxious to have our first rehearsal with "Ex Con," the lead singer, who was a real tall, big guy. All three of us younger guys sang background: Levi did baritone, I was tenor, and John filled out the bass end of the harmony. "Ex Con" learned two or three songs with us, one that everybody knew how to sing, but it wasn't long before Levi and I were exchanging looks, *"Damn, this motherfucker ain't no good."* He was too loud on one song, on another he was too sharp. Some of them were okay, but our general feeling was, *"Let's just get this over with and make some money."*

We knew we looked sharp that night in our rented formal white jackets and black pants. When we hit the stage, we started singing 'Goodnight, Sweetheart, Goodnight' and it sounded nice. The next song was good too. Then we launched into 'My Summer Is Gone' and "Ex Con" started screaming, off-key. He was way over the top with no stage presence. He sounded worse than he did in rehearsal—sharp, flat, and even louder. The manager of the Wolhurst Country Club stood up in the middle of the audience, stopping us after just one verse of the second song. "Hold it!" he shouted. "Get the fuck off my stage and don't come back! Get out! Get out of here!"

Levi and I were so embarrassed. But we looked at each other and knew exactly what the other one was thinking: "*Let's get the hell away from this motherfucker.*" Thank God Barnett had given us a few dollars. We rushed back to the YMCA, grabbed our stuff, and tried to catch a bus home, but it was too late. So we got up the next morning, totally deflated, took our little bags (which were just cleaning bags), and went back to the Greyhound Bus Station. Not until we were on the bus could we finally laugh, wondering how we could have gotten mixed up in such a mess.

Many years later, after the Tops became a popular singing group, we ran into Welton E. Barnett again. He'd moved to California and made an interesting living getting hit by cars and suing for insurance money. He was so proud of his success, as well as ours. He always remembered that he had given Levi and me our first break. "I put y'all in the business," he bragged. And we were grateful that that first catastrophe hadn't discouraged us.

The whole experience in Colorado seemed like a joke. After Levi and I arrived back in Detroit, it was hard to admit to our friends and family that our first professional job had been a total failure, that we had been singing with an amateur ex-convict whose lover hired us to get his career going. I was still faced with the challenge of finding something to do after graduation so I could go to college. I could never have predicted that just two weeks later, Levi and I would be invited to sing at a local graduation party, and this time we would ask two guys who could really sing to join us… Obie Benson and Lawrence Payton.

❧ 2 ❧

The Road Less Traveled

I've always felt it was more than just chance that, out of all the guys Levi and I knew in Detroit who dabbled in singing, we picked Lawrence and Obie. It was like tossing a handful of coins in the air and having them all come up heads. And it all started just because we were thinking about girls. At Pershing High School, there was an elite girls club called the Scheherazades; the prerequisite to membership must have been looking good and being bougie. The head girl, Joanne Artist, was throwing a graduation party in her basement before everyone went off to college in 1954. It was a special occasion, by invitation only, and Joanne asked Levi and I to sing during the party. We eagerly accepted and decided to get two other guys to sing with us; for some reason we thought a group would be better. Lawrence Payton came to mind immediately. We knew he could sing, was good at harmony, and came from a singing family. Plus he looked great, which was mandatory since impressing the girls was essential. Levi's mother and Lawrence's father were cousins so it was like keeping it in the family. Obie Benson we agreed upon too. He had already graduated from high school and was messing around in other singing groups, working and trying to figure out how he was going to get to college. I knew Obie was good, but his singing was really secondary. He had a great personality and was good looking too. We were all about

PERSHING — Doughboys
1952 — 1953

My high school basketball team. I'm player 21.

the same height. Levi and I told them about the party and how fine the girls were. They were both totally down. So we went to the party girl-hunting—singing was the last thing on our minds.

By the middle of the party, the records playing were the popular songs of the day, 'Middle of the Night' by The Clovers and '(Mama) He Treats Your Daughter Mean' by Ruth Brown. Joanne cut off the music and introduced Levi and me, telling everyone that we were great singers. Levi piped up that we had a whole group with us, and she said that was even better. Up to that point we hadn't even thought about what we were going to perform. We all knew that Levi could sing and, whatever he came up with, we'd just improvise and get by. Now we were on the spot, so we went to the side and started whispering, with

Levi saying he was going to do a popular song that he knew.

"Go ahead, man," I said. "We'll back you up." The lyrics went like, *"I'ma sit right down and cry over you."*

Lawrence paused: "Shit, we ain't got no harmony for that." We started getting nervous.

"We'll put something to it," Lawrence said optimistically, his musical instincts kicking in. "Duke, you take the top notes, I got the middle, and Obie, you take the bottom. We gonna start out in unison after Levi sings the first verse."

After less than ten minutes, we were ready. Levi started singing, and then we broke off into a regular three-part harmony. But our voices blended together so well even Levi glanced over at us, *"Motherfuck!"* He just sang the shit out of that song and we kept adding different harmony phrases. Lawrence would lead out high and we just picked up on it right away. It was just beautiful. The girls were screaming, "Wow, y'a'll are great!" Everybody was amazed and we looked at each other, *"Damn!"* It was like we had been rehearsing for two weeks.

Then one of us said, "This should be a group! Can we start rehearsing tomorrow?"

We all said, "Hell *yes!"* The icing on the cake that night was that everybody found a girl, but the most important part was that we found each other.

After the high we experienced at the party, we made a promise to meet at my house the next day and start really rehearsing. Things just fell into place. Lawrence had a musical ear like a composer, and he put the harmonies together. That's when we realized how good he really was. He was born into a musical family from Georgia. As kids growing up on the North End, we'd walk by Lawrence's house and his uncles would be sitting on the porch all day, playing guitar and singing.

After about a week, we must have learned ten to twelve songs of all different genres, from The Four Freshmen to Ray Charles, to The Orioles. Our repertoire drew from the hit parade, be it wonderful ballads like 'How Deep Is the Ocean?' or swinging songs like 'September in the Rain.' It was easy for Lawrence to keep coming up with songs in different harmonies. And we soon realized how good we were at learning them. We also discovered that as much as Levi loved being the lead, he loved singing harmony just as much. He could back off from singing strong leads and blend right in as the fourth voice like a choirboy. For a guy with that kind of fire in his voice to back down and become a smooth-singing choirboy is an incredible talent. It takes a lot of discipline, a lot of knowledge, and a great ear. Fortunately, all of us had great ears.

We could pick up a four-part close harmony almost as well as Lawrence could. Lawrence was inspired by The Four Freshmen, who, along with The Hi-Lo's, were the best at four-part harmonies back then. Other groups would not use it. It's not just the one, three and five notes of a chord scale, which is a normal three-part harmony. It's one, three, five, and part of seven and sometimes nine. It's the fourth note that makes it a four-part harmony. You can move up and down along with the melody note and make four parts. Lawrence got that knowledge from listening to string sessions, and he fashioned our voices after that.

Lawrence could hear a big band arrangement, maybe sixteen pieces, and after one listen he could sing each part in perfect pitch. It was incredible. He could read music and write it, but he'd sing our parts to us. He'd sing mine almost like a trumpet part. Then he'd do the second part which was his, and then the third part which was Levi's. There was no lead back then on some songs; it was just a four-part harmony straight through, similar to The Four Freshmen. Lawrence was a real genius, and we were gifted with an all-star team.

After rehearsing and learning new songs, we were ready to take the next step. Saturday night amateur competitions in Detroit were a big thing for artists and audiences. They gave new talent a chance to showcase their stuff and maybe even win cash prizes. We were still looking to make some money, so we all agreed to try our luck at a competition at the Warfield Theater on Hastings Street. The street was once the heart of Detroit's Paradise Valley where the African American community thrived from the 20s through the 50s. In 1954 the Warfield had the biggest amateur show in town. Even though we had perfected our music, we didn't have matching uniforms, which we knew we needed to look like pros. Still, we managed to pull ourselves together with what we had in our closets and tried not to look too shabby. We weren't sharp but we were determined to look and sing as best we could.

Our first number started out, "*Alright, okay, you win, I'm in love with you,*" then we segued into a shout chorus with a four-part harmony like a trumpet section. The audience jumped to their feet, screaming and clapping because our voices sounded like a brass section. After one more song, we ran off the stage to a standing ovation, which led to us winning the show and being approached by a slick looking guy, who was clearly impressed. "Hey, fellas, what y'all call yourself?" he said, rubbing his hands together.

"We're The Four Aims," one of us piped up with the name we had decided earlier.

"Shit, y'all are good! I think I can get you some work."

"What? Where?" I said, jumping on it. I was aggressive when it came to business. I guess spearheading my school paper drive and being in charge of raising the American flag had been good experience.

"I can get y'all into some nightclubs," he said, sizing us up.

"But we're too young for nightclubs," I hedged.

"Well, y'all look the part. Do you wanna work?" he said, already knowing the answer.

"Yeah, well, we'd like to make some money," I replied, wondering where this was going.

"I tell you what to do," he said, handing us his business card. "My name is Twas. I got a partner named Casablanca. Our agency is Twas and Casablanca."

We almost laughed, that was some funny shit, "Twas and Casablanca." But we kept cool and just stared at the card to make sure we heard it right. We soon learned it was a real agency run by Twas, who was the working agent, and his partner, Casablanca, a pimp who owned an after-hours joint that mostly funded the agency. The agency booked acts primarily on the "Chitlin' Circuit," a group of venues where

African Americans could safely perform during the segregated pre-Civil Rights era. Throughout the country, there were clubs, diners, auditoriums, juke joints, and theaters where Black folks flocked to be entertained by some of the world's greatest performers, from Duke Ellington to Pearl Bailey and Little Richard. The list included nearly every performer of color, including Levi's cousin, Jackie Wilson.

"If you want to get work," Twas explained, "you're gonna need some pictures. We call them lobbies. And you gonna need some uniforms. I'll send the pictures to a few club owners, and as good as y'all look I can get you some work. I'll tell them how good you sing. But just by y'all looking good, I can get you into a club or two."

"Yeah, but how do we get the pictures?" I asked naively.

"Well, y'all gonna have to figure that out yourselves," he said, laughing. It was obvious to him we were new to the game.

Later we talked about it amongst ourselves, and it occurred to me I had a cousin who was a photographer, James E. Bailey. He was so good that he later became the personal photographer of the Henry Ford family of Ford Motors. I made my way over to my aunt's house to ask my cousin for a favor. I told him about our singing group winning at the Warfield and maybe getting our first booking. James knew we didn't have any money, but he was impressed by our big dreams. He agreed to take the pictures, but he also said we needed uniforms.

"You gonna need some good clothes before you take these pictures. Taking pictures with just your faces ain't gonna get it."

"Where are we gonna get these clothes?" I asked again, realizing each step was going to be a hurdle.

"Well, you gonna have to buy them from somewhere, or rent them or whatever," James answered. We talked, and I went back to the group. We decided to ask our family, friends, neighbors, anyone who could help us. Begging for hand-outs, we scraped together a little money and went downtown on a shopping trip.

We headed straight down to Hot Sam's, a men's clothing store that had been around since 1921 and sold the sharpest suits at prices so low folks liked to joke they were stolen. Right away I spotted some white wool suits. I asked Sam Freedman, the owner, if he had four of them. He was a little hesitant. "Yeah, I got 'em. What size?"

"Well, we're all about the same size, my size," I answered, hoping he'd be cooperative.

"Yeah, these cost a little money," he said defensively.

"Well, we've got a little money," I said, talking shit.

Sam got out his tape measure and fitted us up. Meanwhile, we saw some nice white shirts and asked him to fit them up too.

"We don't give credit, you know," he said, anticipating that we didn't have enough for the bill we were racking up.

"We'll figure it out when you add it all up," I said, keenly aware that we couldn't afford it. Then I spotted some blue and white shoes and matching blue and white ties that could set it all off.

Finally, we asked Sam for the bill, which came to about one hundred and fifty dollars. We had one hundred, which was a lot of money for us, but we were still short.

"Listen, Mr. Sam, we have one hundred dollars, but we've got this gig coming up in a couple of weeks. We'll pay you the rest of the money then," I offered.

"See, I told y'all, I knew you was going to ask that shit," he shook his head. "I don't do no credit."

"Look man, this ain't really credit. You're just letting us have these suits so we can we make some money. We ain't trying to pay two, three, ten dollars a week. We're gonna pay you all at once right after the weekend. We've just got to have these suits."

We just kept talking, begging him. Finally, for some reason, he broke down.

"I'll tell you what," he said, "you look honest enough. I gonna let you have them. You don't look like the kind of guys who are trying to beat me out of anything. But you are going to owe me. Fifty-two dollars and some change. And if you don't bring me my money, I'll find your asses, and I'll put y'all in jail."

We were so thrilled we could have hugged him.

"I swear on the Bible," I said, "as soon as we get this money we gonna bring it to you."

And we did. The Monday morning after our first gig, I went down to Hot Sam's and gave him his money. He was so pleased. Years later his daughter saw me somewhere and told me that her dad always talked about us. He was so glad that he let us have those outfits when we first started out. It was one of the best things he'd ever done. He'd never given credit to anyone. But he was very thankful he helped us. And he felt like he'd played a big part in our success, which he did. "I was the first one who dressed y'all in the business," he said. He just loved The Four Tops.

With Hot Sam's help, we knew we were looking good in our cool white uniforms. I called my cousin to tell him we were ready for our photo shoot. He took some great "lobbies" for us, probably named for the black-and-white publicity photos of celebrities and entertainers that lined the entryways and corridors of movie theaters and palaces, restaurants, and studios in the 40s and 50s. We called Twas and he wanted to see them right away.

"Oh, man, these are great!" he said. "I'm about to get you all some work."

About three days later, he called me. At the beginning, I was the guy out in front, driving us forward, not taking no for an answer. I had the energy and the get-up-and-go, probably a lot of nerve, plus a dream. Twas came through with a three-night gig at Eddie's Lounge, in Flint, Michigan, an hour's drive from Detroit. He said he'd drive us back and forth the sixty mile commute each night, pay for the gas and take a ten per cent agent fee from the two hundred dollar booking. We'd split the rest four ways after we subtracted what we owed Hot Sam for our uniforms. We would have done the gig for nothing.

"You're going to have to do about five songs each show, and you are opening up for a shake dancer called Tequila Wallace."

This was another first for us. Sexy women dancing, shaking, and stripping down to a bare minimum was the usual opening act on the Chitlin' Circuit, and we were well on the road.

"Y'all do the best you can," Twas told us, "because if you do good, I got more work for you."

Even though we had been learning several songs, we added a few more, and made sure we had some smooth moves for the stage. We were flying by the seat of our pants since we had no sheet music. Before we went onstage, Lawrence went to the piano player and told him what key the songs were in. The band was a rhythm section with a couple of horn players. We started off with a song by The Midnighters, 'Work with Me Annie,' then followed that up with 'September in the Rain' and 'How Deep Is the Ocean?'

The audience didn't know what to expect. At first, they just listened, checking us out. Pretty soon they started clapping and seemed like they were in seventh heaven. We were singing our butts off, looking at each other and laughing. Levi's years of singing in his childhood paid off; he had great stage presence and the audience was in the palm of his hands. We just went along with his mastery. By the time we ran offstage, wrapping it up with our own version of 'Alright, Okay, You Win,' a real hot song back then, people were out of their seats giving us a standing ovation. The applause was ringing in our ears as Twas met us backstage, letting us know he was going to get us more work right then and there.

After he left, we just looked at each other and started talking all at once. We knew that this was what we wanted to do, and nothing else. We loved it!

Obie said what we were all thinking: "Shit, we can make money. We're as good as anybody out there. Forget what we were trying before, we should be doing this." In unison, we all agreed.

The next engagement Twas booked for us was in Cleveland, Ohio, at a club called the Ebony Lounge. One week at four hundred dollars, a big bump for us, but this time we had to find a way to get there and a place to stay. We had a friend who believed in us and was kind enough to drive us to Cleveland. But we had no idea how to get a room. When we arrived, the only people at the club were the musicians, the bandleader, and the rhythm section, waiting for the owner to come. The bandleader spotted us right away, walking in like we didn't know where we were.

"Y'all the new act? The Four Aims?"

We nodded. That was the name we stuck with. We really were aiming for the stars.

"We heard you're pretty good singers."

We said thanks, asking him where we could get a room and how much it would cost.

The bandleader shrugged. "You need to go talk to Dan Boone," he told us, referring to the owner. "About where y'all gonna stay and whatever else."

"Hey, man, we ain't got a dime. How do we get food?" I asked. We had our pride, but we hadn't eaten all day.

"Why don't you ask him for an advance?" he suggested.

"What's that?" I asked. That's how young and inexperienced we were.

"An advance on the money he is going to pay you. He might give you enough money to check into a hotel and get something to eat."

That sounded good, so we sat down to wait along with the band. We started talking, and they quickly discovered that we didn't have our own musical arrangements on paper.

"If y'all know your songs, we can get them together for you," he offered, trying to help us out.

Lawrence told him the songs we wanted to sing, 'This Can't Be Love,' 'In the Still of the Night,' and 'The Nearness of You.'

He said, "Damn, y'all sing these songs?"

We knew this wasn't the usual Black repertoire. Most of our songs were standards.

From the time we started, one of the first things we agreed upon was that we didn't want to be a group like The Midnighters, The Orioles, or The Clovers, all admired R&B groups of the day who sang to Black people and in Black venues exclusively. We felt that we could sing any kind of song and work anywhere. We weren't trying not to be Black, we were just trying to be as good as any group in the business. At that time, The Ink Spots and The Mills Brothers were the only two crossover groups who appealed to both Black and white audiences. They'd set the bar, but we thought we could do even better.

To add to our list of standards, we told him that we also sang a couple of really funky songs, 'Alright, Okay, You Win,' 'What I'd Say,' and 'Sh-Boom,' which was on the hit parade at the time. It wasn't too funky, but we made it sound good.

"Tell you what," he said, nodding with encouragement. "I can write you some piano parts to these songs. I can have these done for tonight. And I'll tell my rhythm section what to do," he said.

Dan, the owner, finally arrived and we introduced ourselves.

"Y'all pretty set for the show tonight?" he asked, checking us out. We knew that Twas had given us a really big build up.

We told him that we were getting it together. The bandleader was writing our arrangements. We just had one uniform, but we could wash our shirts every night.

"But look, man, I don't know how to ask you," I said while the other guys held their breath. "But we ain't got no money to eat or to check in to a hotel."

"Okay," he said without missing a beat, reaching in his pocket. "I can give you an advance. Here's one hundred dollars."

Our eyes lit up. He told us to go to the Collingwood, the hotel where most of the colored performers stayed. It was small but it didn't cost much. Ten dollars a room per week. He called ahead to let them know we were checking in. Nearby was a good restaurant where we could eat breakfast, lunch, and dinner.

"Y'all, go ahead, check in and feed your skinny asses," he said. We really were thin.

We took the money and almost ran straight to the restaurant where we sat down and ate for hours. Then we went to the hotel, rested and freshened up. We all lived in separate rooms, barely big enough to fit in, but at least we each had our own space. The Collingwood had no air conditioning though, so we opened the windows and breathed in the fresh air, relaxing for the first time in hours. We felt as good as if we were staying in a five-star hotel.

When we arrived back at the Ebony Lounge, a shake dancer was gyrating and shimmying on the floor. She was the opening act, and we were the closing one. When we took to the stage, immediately we could hear the "ohhs" and "ahhs" in the audience. The way we looked—our matching attire and us being young and good-looking (I didn't put on the glasses I'd worn since I was fourteen because I wanted us all to look alike)—was the first thing that hit them. Levi used to say, "It's called, getting 'em." That night we "got 'em" and we were so excited.

When we started performing, we kept hearing people exclaim, "These guys can really sing!" They were amazed that we sounded like The Four Freshmen with the same beautiful harmonies. It was the era where vocalists started being featured, rather than bands and instrumentals. People enjoyed hearing four young Black guys who could sing songs like 'In the Still of the Night,' which Della Reese had just put out, 'This Can't Be Love,' and 'How Deep Is the Ocean.' We were also singing Ray Charles' funky songs peppered in with the pretty stuff. It was a great mixture, unique on the Chitlin' Circuit. We weren't concentrating on selling records. We wanted to be live entertainers and follow in the footsteps Sammy Davis, Barbara McNair, and a few others who were able to climb that ladder of success without having hit records.

After our successful opening night, we went back to our little hotel rooms. I couldn't wait to call my mom to share the good news. I was so excited and dialed her on the pay phone down the hall. She didn't know I had been singing since I'd left home after graduation. I didn't mention it or that the four of us had been living with Obie.

"Hi, Mom," I said. "I'm in Cleveland, singing with The Four Aims."

"The Four Aims? Who's that?"

"It's my group, we're going to the top. We're aiming for the stars."

"You singing that devil's music?" She was so mad she almost came through the phone. "No good can come of it." "Mama, it ain't devil's music. We're singing pretty songs and people love it."

"Dukie, you singing the devil's music and you know it. You know you should be here working or going to school. You got that college scholarship, plus you took those tests and applied for all those different jobs. They wrote you back letters saying you can work for the city, or you can work for the state."

"Mama, I'm doing what I know I should do. You know I love music."

"Son, if you was here, I would beat your butt, you know that."

I was happy I was a hundred miles away, because I knew she would have. There was a long pause. I felt bad that I had disappointed her and made her so unhappy. I wondered if she was crying. I was relieved when she finally spoke again. "I tell you what, you remember how to pray?"

"Yes, Mama."

"I want you to go to whatever room by yourself and pray

to the Lord. And I guarantee you, Dukie, he'll tell you what to do and what not to do. Promise me you'll do what he tells you."

"Okay, Mama," I agreed, heartbroken because I thought she would enjoy hearing that I was making money using my God-given talent.

I hung up and went back to my room, thinking sadly about everything she said. Because I promised, I said a prayer and fell asleep praying. In my sleep I had the most beautiful, clear, and vivid dream.

The four of us were singing, dressed in silver silk jackets and black ties, dressed to the bone. We were as sharp as anybody in show business. The song we were singing was a big hit, catchy and swinging with a great beat and a tremendous melody. It went on and on. Then all of a sudden—BAM. A loud crash cut the dream off. I woke up to see that the window next to my bed had slammed shut.

I sat up, half awake, half asleep, but the dream was still in my head. I knew the Lord had just given me my answer. I ran down the hall and started knocking on the guys' doors. I woke everyone up and we met in the hallway. I told them about the dream, how powerful it was. As I described it to them, I was so emotional they cried. Deep in our hearts, we all knew we could really sing. We had that kind of confidence. We were as good as any group we'd heard, but it was more than that. We'd seen the effect we had on people. That was something special. The guys all gathered around and embraced me.

"Duke had this dream. We're gonna make it." We hugged

each other and made a pact that night to stick together no matter what. A pact that was never broken.

Naturally, we had no idea of the tests that we'd face along the way. It didn't matter how much confidence we had in our ability, soon we were about to receive a major lesson in humility. Despite growing up in a city where great singing could be heard in every bar and on every street corner, nothing could have prepared us for the shock we'd experience when we encountered a dazzling, outrageous entertainer, booked in the same venue. He blew us out of the water.

❧ 3 ❧

The Road To Idlewild

It was 1955, about a year had passed and Twas kept his word. Our bookings kept getting bigger and better. We were thrilled to be playing at clubs and venues on the Chitlin' Circuit throughout the South. After a while, he landed us our best gig so far, the Royal Peacock in Atlanta, with a reputation as one of the best clubs in the country. We'd be staying at the only decent place Blacks could stay in Atlanta, the Savoy Hotel, which was owned by B.B. Beamon, a former Pullman porter, and a big guy in the insurance business. He owned the Royal Peacock and he also owned the hotel right down the street from the club.

By the time we stepped off the Greyhound Bus in the Atlanta terminal we were exhausted, ready to go straight to the hotel. The guys went to find our luggage while I looked for a bathroom. By then we had three uniforms, the white one from Hot Sam's, a brown set, and a cheaper suit that was bright blue; it was all we could afford, but it looked nice onstage. We used cleaning bags for our luggage (not the plastic kind; they were made of heavy brown wrapping paper), but still we felt like "travelling pros."

I stepped into the first waiting room I could find and walked inside. As soon as I did someone pushed up next to me, and I felt cold, hard steel pressed up against my skull. Out of the corner of my eye, I could see a white man wearing some kind of a badge.

"Hey, boy, get the fuck out of here!" he said in a vicious Southern drawl. I froze. "Get your Black ass out of here!"

Then a little old white lady butted in, pointing, "The 'colored' waiting room is down the hall. Hurry, go, he might kill you!"

I backed away while the irate white man kept screaming. "Get the fuck out of here! Go on nigger get! Get!"

"Okay, okay," I managed to say as I stumbled away, "I'm going." I ran back out to the guys, babbling on about what had just happened, warning them not to go in that direction. We found a small, funky waiting room in another part of the terminal with a nasty water fountain and a "colored" sign over it. We tried not to stay there but two seconds. Then as fast as we could we got a cab and went straight to the hotel.

That was our first introduction to Atlanta. I've always wondered what would have happened if that old white lady hadn't said something. What if I'd lost my cool? Was she another one of the angels in my life? Whoever she was, I'm glad she spoke up.

We headed to the club soon after arriving at the hotel, since Beamon had informed us we could eat there and also we had to rehearse. The first thing we noticed was another name on the marquee, the opening act, "James Brown and his Famous Flames." "Who's that?" we said. The name of his new recording, 'Please, Please, Please,' was listed too. We were curious about him, but we got busy rehearsing with the band and didn't think more about it. Instead we concentrated on running through our songs.

By now we had some nice arrangements on paper: a guitar

part and a piano part. From that you could do almost anything. We still didn't have any horn arrangements, but wherever we played there were usually two or three horns that could pick up riffs and add to it. All the musicians were pretty good at improvising back then. The band was elated that we were singing old standards and jazz type songs in this Chitlin' Circuit club. We discovered that people really enjoyed good singing as long as you gave them some funk every now and then. After rehearsal we went back to the hotel. We'd still hadn't heard the other act and didn't give it much thought.

By the time we got back to the club, the Friday night crowd packed the house. The place was jumping. We went down to our dressing room to get ready, where we could hear the M.C. announcing, "Ladies and Gentlemen, Mr. James Brown." So we kind of crept upstairs to see what this James Brown was all about. All of sudden his band blasted out this funky music, and he started dancing and singing a mile a minute. We were amazed. He was tearing up the house. "*Shit!*" It was phenomenal.

All of a sudden we panicked. "Why in the world would they have us follow *him*? This man's even got a record—he's doing it!"

We just kept looking at him; it was hard to tear our eyes away. Then slowly we backed down the stairs and kept listening, disbelieving that he could maintain this fever pitch for about twenty-five more minutes. All we could do was look at each other thinking, "*How in the fuck we gone follow this?*"

We were getting scared, to be honest. Not only was he sharp, he was moving faster than lightning. His little band was tight, moving in unison, horns blowing; it was unbelievable. Nothing like it. We sat there thinking and almost praying. At the end of his act, it got quiet. We looked around, speechless for a minute, then I squeaked out, "Well, what we gonna do fellas?"

Levi finally spoke up. "Well, ain't but one thing we can do. First of all, we going to go up there and tell the manager to take an extra fifteen minute intermission. Instead of fifteen it's going to be a half hour. We gonna have to cool these folks off." We nodded, good idea.

He went on, "We can't out funk him, we can't out dance him, we can't out holler him, but we can out sing this motherfucker. So we just gonna go up there and sing. That's the only chance we've got. We can add a little funk in there, but we gotta come out there singing and looking debonair and just sing to the ladies. That's all we can do. That's us."

When the M.C. finally introduced our act—"Presenting the Four Aims!"—it was one of the first times I was nervous; I was shaking and shit. We started out singing 'This Can't Be Love.' Obie was singing lead, sounding like Nat King Cole. People started quieting down, listening. When we got to the chorus, we were singing in four-part harmony, and the crowd just lit up. People started going "whoah" and clapping. Then we started dancing, throwing in some slick, cool moves, getting them in the groove. Now the girls were really checking us out. After that Levi slowed it all the way down, singing 'How Deep Is the Ocean?' a beautiful love ballad. He had them right in the palm of his hand. We then did two or three up-tempo numbers and ended with 'Alright, Okay, You Win' which had a big shout chorus. Off we ran, leaving the stage to a standing ovation.

We couldn't have been happier or more relieved when we talked about the show back at the hotel. We agreed that whenever we came up against anybody doing their thing, all we had to remember was to *do our thing*, the best way we could. That was our conclusion. The only way you are going to win is just by being yourself.

Our encounter with James Brown intimidated us at first but it made us work even harder. We started learning new songs every week. Songs like 'Work with Me Annie' were hot at that time, and we added that to our repertoire. And new funkier, bluesier songs, 'Fever' by Little Willie John, and 'Grits Ain't Groceries.' We ended up feeling really felt good about our Royal Peacock engagement. And it was not the last time our paths would cross with James Brown's across the country. All our careers were taking off when we first met and along the way we'd trade stories and give each other advice as we climbed the ladder.

Several years later, James made a point to pay us a visit later on in our careers, when the Tops were appearing in a club in Cherry Hill, New Jersey. After the show he came to the dressing room and started right in.

"Y'all still playing in these nightclubs?" he asked. "You know, to stay in the game you have to do more one nighters. That's how you make real money."

My reply was, "Nah, man, the way you stay in this business is you book engagements in nightclubs. And do some one-nighters. That shit will carry you forever. "

He shook his long processed, slicked-back mane. "Look at me, man, I'm just gonna do the one-night gigs. That's it."

So we talked and argued about which way to go, sitting there drinking brandy and talking shit until six in the morning. By the time we left we were both loaded. His parting words were, "Okay, we gonna see who wins." And I said, "Yeah, we gonna see who wins."

As time went by, with all of our individual ups and downs, we would always check in on each other. One time, after years of the Tops staying on top of the game doing nightclub engagements, James said, "Shit, I guess what you said was alright."

I replied, "I guess what you said was alright too, James. Looks like we're both winning."

He laughed and said, "Fuck it, let's just keep doing our thang. Y'all good at what you do, that's one thing." But he was way past us by then; James Brown was playing on every R&B radio station throughout the country, the "Godfather of Soul." We were big Motown artists and to the public we may have seemed pretty much on the same level, but we never made his kind of money. James was one of a kind. We always liked him a lot, and he liked us too.

After our Royal Peacock gig we worked in a couple of clubs owned by another prominent Black entrepreneur, Arthur George Gaston. Eventually, we wound up back in Detroit. Word was getting out, our reputation was growing—"*These motherfuckers can sing! They're great onstage and they look good too!*" We were proud to be gaining popularity in our hometown and working every weekend at the Roosevelt Lounge, the Rage Show Bar, or the Flame Show Bar. We were especially proud that we kept getting bookings without ever releasing a record. By then we would have loved to record but our initial goal, as we told James, was to have careers like the entertainers performing in Vegas or New York, like Frank Sinatra, Nat King Cole, and Sammy Davis. We had successfully broken into the Chitlin' Circuit, but true to our name we were aiming for something higher. Surprisingly, it didn't take much longer for an important part of our plan to materialize.

We were back in Detroit working an industry event, the yearly Auto Show, which showcased new model cars and live entertainment for the crowd. We had just come off stage from performing in the late afternoon when Twas, who was now more like a manager than simply a booking agent, came us to us really hyped. "Hey, Duke, guess what? This big numbers guy, Arthur Braggs, owns a club up in Idlewild, Michigan. He's interested in coming to see y'all. You ever heard of him?"

I told him that I had. I was lying.

"Braggs's got a great club, orchestra, dancing girls, show girls, all that kind of stuff. If he likes you, you can work up there all summer."

"Oh man, all summer! We've been looking for something like that!"

The next day at the Auto Show we sang four or five songs in our beautiful uniforms. We had added a few new ones by then and always dressed impeccably with show business flare, never over the top. They were cheap but looked impressive onstage.

When we came off stage, a good-looking, muscular man about five foot eight, dressed to the nines, self-assured and magnetic, caught our eye. It was Arthur Braggs. By then we had done our homework about him. We knew that he was a promoter/ hustler/entrepreneur/numbers man who had become a well-regarded producer of first-rate entertainment. He worked with only the best singers, dancers, and musicians, booking them in a club he leased in the exclusive Black summer resort known as Idlewild. The resort was two hundred miles north of Detroit, situated on a beautiful lake surrounded by pine trees and charming cottages. It sounded like paradise.

"Fellas!" Arthur Braggs said, as he approached us, shaking our hands. "I like the way y'all sang! And you look good too. I think you Four Aims have a great future."

This was music to our ears. We tried to stay cool, thanking him profusely.

"Listen, I'm interested in having y'all come to Idlewild, you ever heard of it?"

I nodded yes, but he could probably see I needed schooling.

"An all-Negro summer resort, top shelf, first class all the way. I own a nightclub up there, where I produce a real nice show called the Idlewild Revue. How about I bring you up for a weekend and if you do well, I'll keep you for the rest of the summer. Two months' work. It's a good three hours' drive from Detroit. Y'all got a ride?"

I said no, but he didn't miss a beat.

"Then I'll send for y'all. Even got a place for you to stay, right across from the club. You have to pay for it, hardly nothing.

The Idlewild Club House, Michigan, where we performed early in our career.
ROBERT ABBOTT SENGSTACKE/GETTY

Rehearsals start the day before we open July 4th weekend, make sure you get there early. Anything you need, give me a call."

We were so happy we could have hugged him. "Yes, sir, Mr. Braggs, thank you." Later we learned that everyone called him Daddy Braggs. We felt his protective, caring quality from the start.

We couldn't wait to get to Idlewild and counted the days until his driver came to get us. After a relaxing drive through upper Michigan's rural parkland setting, we arrived bright-eyed and ready to work. We checked into the rooming house Mr. Braggs secured for us, right across the road from the Paradise Club.

They assigned us to one big bedroom like a dormitory. There were two beds pushed together, and room for just one dresser, but we had our own bathroom and no complaints about our no-frills, camp-like accommodations. The idea that we could spend the summer working in such a historic, unique setting was amazing.

Idlewild had been around since 1912 when four white couples purchased a parcel of land to establish a vacation community for African Americans during segregation, when Blacks weren't able to enjoy the same outdoor leisure and recreation facilities that whites did. By the time Arthur Braggs took over the lease for the Paradise Club, the resort had grown and flourished under Black ownership for close to fifty years. The setting was idyllic, with mostly small homes and cottages nestled beside crystal clear lakes and majestic pine trees. There were only a few businesses and establishments throughout its over two thousand acres: a club house, hotel, one church, a community hall, a post office, and a grocery store with a gas station fueling pump. There were two clubs in town, the Flamingo Bar and the Paradise Nightclub, where we were booked in the Fiesta Room. We were thrilled and right away we prayed that Daddy Braggs would ask us to stay the whole summer.

By the time we got to the club for our first rehearsal, there were already people onstage warming up, milling around sizing each other up. Big, tall, beautiful showgirls. Smaller girls as cute as could be, dancing around. A gay dancer in his own world flying all over the stage. A big, goofy guy tap dancing along with two short, little guys called the Harlem Brothers who were doing athletic flips. It was a great mix.

We traded glances with each other. "*This is going to be interesting.*"

Rehearsals began with the opening number performed by cute young girls known as the Ziggy Johnson dancers. They were very professional, having trained at a prestigious dancing school in Detroit. They had been hand-selected, and were still underage high school girls, but you couldn't tell from their level of talent and ability. We were like *damn*. They must have been the best dancers in the school. As we watched the entire rehearsal, we realized that each one of the performers could wow an audience. All eyes were on us when it was our turn to run through our numbers.

As we made our way onstage, we handed the bandleader our lead sheets. He passed them to the leader of the horn section, which was made up of about five or six horns. He glanced at our arrangements, which were just for the piano and rhythm section, and raised his eyebrows.

"Look, I'm going to write y'all some horn parts, because I got these horns over here, and they can read music. They need something to play too."

"It's gonna cost us?" Obie said, probably hoping it would play out like when we got our last charts for free.

"I have to charge you," he said, sizing us up. "I know y'a'll have to have it."

"Naw, we don't really need them," I wanted to bargain with him. We didn't have much cash. "We're just gonna be here for one week."

"Well, from what I heard, I bet y'all be here the whole summer. So I'll make you a deal, you can pay me as you go along." His name was Walter "Choker" Campbell and, unknowingly, he bolstered our confidence betting that we'd be around for the duration of the summer.

The band started playing our charts without the horns, while those arrangements were being written. We began singing 'In the Still of the Night' and the noise in the background started quieting down. All eyes opened wide and folks stopped moving around. We were singing like The Four Freshmen in impeccable harmony. Then we moved into 'Alright, Okay.' After that, 'What a Difference a Day Makes,' just like Dinah Washington did, with the *ohh's* flowing in a heavenly harmony, underscoring the lyrics.

"...*It's heaven when you find romance on your menu, what a difference a day makes, and the difference is you.*"

Of course, Levi's delivery was just remarkable. We could hear the girls swooning "ohh" and "ahh." He knocked everyone out.

Daddy Braggs met us behind the curtain as we danced off stage, wiping the sweat off our brows. We'd worked even harder than usual trying to impress him. "Looks like you guys are going to be here all summer. I think you're going to be great in my show." He immediately jumped into choreographing his vision from start to finish, weaving us into the entire show.

"As the show starts I want you all to come out with the girls dancing around you. You'll sing the opening number with the girls, 'There's No Business Like Show Business.'"

I was blown away. "Shit," I said, "this is Las Vegas stuff."

"Shit, that's what I do." He said, laughing, like he'd planned this routine the whole time.

We started learning new songs and Mr. Braggs was delighted to discover how easily we could pick up dance moves and choreography. The showgirls would walk around and prance during certain numbers, but the Ziggy Johnson dancers did the serious performing. They started with the opening number, performed another one in the middle and almost before they could change and catch their breath, they'd be back again, wrapping it up in the show's big finale. Braggs's show was based around the three numbers. Opening, middle, and closing.

After that first opening weekend, major headliners were added to the revue. The house was packed every weekend. Not just Black folks came, most times whites would outnumber them in the audience. Word spread and folks from the neighboring areas, Muskegon, Traverse City, Grand Rapids, would come up to see this wonderful class act at the Paradise Club. Lawyers, doctors, teachers, factory workers, plumbers— everyone just checked their prejudices at the door and mingled together to enjoy the music. Some members of the audience owned private lake houses in the area, others would come up and rent cabins for the weekend. There was a real party going on all the time.

The family feeling in the audience extended to the performers too. Especially the special connection that developed rapidly between The Four Aims and the young Ziggy Johnson dancers. On the way to our dressing room during the show, we had to cross through the girls' dressing room, and we often saw them half-naked, changing costumes. Even though we tried to be as professional as possible, we couldn't help but get turned on. Clineice, Inez, Donna, and Valaida were just seventeen or eighteen that first summer, and we weren't much older. It seemed like they were as hot and bothered as we were.

Word came down from Daddy Braggs and Ziggy Johnson, the show's M.C., that we were not to mess with these girls. We assured everyone that we just wanted to be friends, but we kept getting eyes from the girls. They told us about a club about a mile away called Wonderland, where Idlewilders hung out after the show to unwind. They invited us to come the night after we opened. Everyone would be there, even Daddy Braggs and Ziggy Johnson. Of course, they would be accompanied by their chaperone. The only way Ziggy Johnson could convince their parents to let them leave home and work in a nightclub for the summer was if they were under constant supervision. Their parents didn't want them messing around with the musicians. Unfortunately, that was the category we fell under, so we knew we had to be gentlemanly at all times. But in spite of all the watchful eyes and us trying our best to exhibit gentlemanly behavior, we kept getting closer and closer.

During the day we would ease over to the girls' cabin, and they would cook for us. We'd buy groceries and they'd make a big pot of something, good old home cooking, and we'd sit around eating and getting to know each other. Sometimes we would meet at the beach. There was a little cove about half a mile up the road from the Paradise Club. We would stretch out on beach blankets, swim, sun, and listen to music on transistor radios. It was the perfect backdrop for falling in love.

When it was just the guys, we would play baseball, basketball, tennis, go fishing—just good clean fun. We didn't have to work every night of the week and on our nights off, I'd hang around Daddy Braggs, watching him manage the club. He was a role model to me. I noted how he used a clicker to count the number of people who came in, making sure that the money collected at the door money wasn't short. One day he took notice that I was constantly underfoot.

"You trying to learn something, ain't you, Duke?"

I guessed he was right, nodding, "Yeah, I think it's pretty cool." After that, he took a special interest in me. Since my days doing the school paper drive, I was always interested in running a business. Mr. Braggs helped me understand show business on another level. I seemed to have a knack for numbers; I had automatically taken care of the group's payroll from the start. Everyone in the group contributed in a different way. We each sort of fell into our natural roles, and we were comfortable with them.

* * *

By the end of the summer, everyone in the whole revue had become very friendly. We were like a big family. On Labor Day, in the final show of the season, there was a tradition called "Burying the Show." All the performers would do someone else's part. Our group would try to perform like the dancing girls. We even did our best to dress like them in girly costumes.

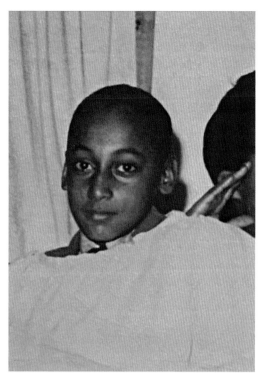

My parents, Nazim Ali Fakir and Rubyleon Eckridge, on their wedding day, 1930.

Ready for family choir practice, mid-40s.

With my elder siblings, 1936. (L–R) Alladhi, Shazen, me, and Azim.

With fellow students of Hutchins Middle School at our graduation, 1946. I was class Vice President.

Learning our four-part harmonies, 1963.

Looking sharp in matching suits and shoes, 1964. (L–R) Me, Lawrence, Levi, and Obie.

Rehearsing our choreography in the basement of the Apollo Theatre, New York City, 1964.
MICHAEL OCHS ARCHIVES/GETTY

Enjoying the view from a New York rooftop.
MICHAEL OCHS ARCHIVES/GETTY

The Four Tops, 1965.
MICHAEL OCHS ARCHIVES/GETTY

Performing 'Standing in the Shadows of Love' on
Britain's *Ready Steady Go*, 1966.
BIPS/GETTY

Exploring London, 1966.
PICTORIAL PRESS LTD/ALAMY

Backstage at London's Saville Theatre, where we played the last night of the tour arranged by Brian Epstein, 1966.
MIRRORPIX

Perfecting the Four Tops look, 1966.
MOTOWN RECORDS

Meeting Princess Margaret with Mary Wilson, 1971.
STEVE WOOD/DAILY EXPRESS/GETTY

Performing with Aretha Franklin, 1972.
PICTORIAL PRESS LTD/ALAMY

Piper and me on our wedding day, with our mothers, 1974.

Seventies chic, 1976.

All smiles backstage, 1985.

They would sing our parts, putting on our uniforms, rolling up the pants past their waists, trying to wear our shoes. It was the funniest thing you've ever seen, with every act switching up roles. A show within a show. People from the area loved it, the last show sold out each year. It was a great way to wind up the season with a bang.

That first summer in Idlewild was so new and exciting, with us learning so much about life and show business, I can't imagine a better experience for young singers starting their careers. We were looked after by a great Black producer in a safe, idyllic environment, where every two weeks a different great artist would be headlining. It was a dream come true. One week we'd work with the legendary Jackie Wilson. The next week it would be Brook Benton or Della Reese, and many more. Mr. Braggs had a special relationship with Della. She was a good friend of his for quite some time. He even bought her a pink convertible, Thunderbird, which she looked fabulous in. His generosity extended to us, too. By the end of that summer, he had purchased us our own wood-paneled Plymouth station wagon, complete with a record player. We were walking on air up in Idlewild; even though I had had that prophetic dream about us attaining success, this was a step I could never have dreamed of.

The other amazing, totally unforeseen occurrence was that each of us found love at the same time, in the same place, like a fairy tale romance. Four brothers falling in love with four sisters, that's how bonded we were. The magic from that Idlewild summer of 1955 carried over to Detroit when the show was over. No matter how much everyone tried to discourage our romantic friendships, writing them off as summer flings, they continued when we got back home in the fall. The four cool cat singers seriously started dating the four young dancers. I began regularly going down to the Ziggy Johnson School of Dance to have lunch with Inez. Obie stepped it up with Val, taking her out on real dates. Levi would go to Clineice's house to spend time with her and get to know her family. Lawrence was pursuing a serious relationship with Donna. This wasn't just messing around; we were seriously courting. The folks who thought we were just four jive entertainers without serious intentions must have been surprised when Obie, Levi and I married our lovely Ziggy Johnson dancers. Only Lawrence, after years of dating Donna, wed someone else.

In the relationship area, I seemed to move faster than my other brothers and after our second summer in Idlewild, during one of our breaks from touring, I married Inez. She was a nice young lady, and her parents welcomed me into their family. As a performer, I was still an unproven commodity in Detroit. Guys like me were a dime a dozen, an aspiring entertainer without a certain future, but they must have taken my love for her and my sincerity into account. We had our wedding at her parent's house on Vicksburg near Linwood on the west side of Detroit. It was a very simple wedding, officiated by her priest, with my family and the other Tops in attendance. Even though it was a happy occasion there was a somber aspect for me. My grandmother, the one who had imparted her values to me about discipline and hard work, was very ill and couldn't attend our ceremony. My grandfather had passed away a few months earlier. She was living by herself and my mother asked if Inez and I would stay with her for a while after we married. My grandmother told her that even though I was a man, I would always be her baby. She welcomed Inez and me into her home, where we spent the early part of our married life when I wasn't on the road. About a year later, my grandmother passed away. Around the same time, Inez and I were blessed with a baby girl, Kai. Now it wasn't just me—I had a family to take care of. If I wasn't motivated before, I was more passionate than ever about reaching the top.

❧ 4 ❧
The Road To Recording

If our success was somehow a part of a bigger plan, with God blessing us with the gift of song and laying the groundwork for us to find each other, there were also helping hands along the way. People in our lives were angels too. Of course, Daddy Braggs became a father figure and an angel when he took us under his wing. But it was Lawrence's cousin, Roquel "Billy" Davis, who paved the way to our first recording.

Billy actually acted in the capacity of The Four Aims' unofficial manager soon after we first started out. Once we began travelling regularly, booking gigs throughout the country, Lawrence's grandmother insisted that Billy come along to help promote us and do behind-the-scenes legwork. Like almost all of Lawrence's family, he was musically gifted. A talented songwriter, he had collaborated with another up-and-coming songwriter from Detroit, Berry Gordy Jr. The two wrote hit songs for Davis' second cousin, Jackie Wilson, among them 'To Be Loved' and 'Lonely Teardrops.' However, their writing partnership was eclipsed by Gordy's entrepreneurial vision. He went off to start his own record company. Billy was offered a chance to join Chess Records as a vice president. He took us along with him. Because of Billy they agreed to record four songs he had written for us.

So off we went to Chicago and our first recording session.

Dining with Billy Davis, who was a great early supporter. Levi's first left, I'm fourth from left, Lawrence and Billy are center, Obie's third from right.

Before the session Phil and Leonard Chess came downstairs to deal with the band. The Chess brothers had a big company in the 50s, recording Black rock 'n' rollers, Chuck Berry, Muddy Waters, Howlin' Wolf, Etta James, and Bo Diddley, among others. As the meeting began, they turned to us: "Hey, fellas, before you record, you're going to have to change your name."

We were caught completely off guard. They continued breaking it down; apparently they had given this a lot of thought. "You call yourselves The Four Aims, but there's already a group out there, the Ames Brothers, spelled A-m-e-s. They're a white group, but we can't have The Four Aims coming out of Chess even if it's spelled different."

I protectively jumped in. "I think people will know the difference."

But it was clear their minds were already made up. 'Well, we just can't have that. You have to change your name." Case closed.

We looked at each other, totally unprepared, but we immediately started brainstorming.

"Well, we were aiming for the stars. Shooting for the moon. We want to be on top. To signify what we're trying to do."

The music director chimed in, "What about The Four Tops?"

That rang a bell. So that's when The Four Tops were born, in 1956 at Chess Records. That day we recorded the four songs Billy had written, and they released one single. The A-side of the 45 was 'Kiss Me Baby,' but deejays liked the B-side, 'Could It Be You.' It didn't sell a thing. We didn't really have a deal with Chess, so that was the end of that.

Not having a hit record didn't stop our momentum. Even though we had been rechristened as The Four Tops by a respected record label, we were still more into live singing and performing. In the 50s, if your live act was good enough you could make it in the world of entertainment. We still believed that we were as good as the Mills Brothers. We could sing the kind of songs that people loved to hear in showrooms, supper clubs, dance halls, or performing arts centers. We kept up learning those kinds of songs. Our repertoire was vast since we had the ability to learn a song in half a day. While we sat around waiting for gigs, we were always singing and rehearsing.

Feeling like we were beginning to hit our stride, we decided to go to the Mecca of show business, New York City, find a place to stay, and look for work however long it took to get a break. Somewhere along the way, we'd met a drummer, a nice Jewish guy, and his mother happened to manage an apartment building on 59th Street. She rented us a studio apartment with one Murphy pullout bed on the wall—that was all. The first night we got there, we looked around our new apartment and started laughing.

"Well, let's flip a coin to see who gets to sleep in the bed first, the rest of us can hit the floor." Staring at the hard wood floor without a carpet chased away the thrill of having our own place in New York.

Lawrence had heard that Earl Garner, the virtuoso jazz pianist who often vocalized while he played, was appearing at Birdland. We loved jazz and Birdland was the home to legendary performers like Charlie "Yardbird" Parker and John Coltrane, so off we went to enjoy the show.

Seeing Earl Garner play in person was amazing and when he finished his set, he told the audience he was going to rest up before the second show. Savoring his drink, Lawrence looked around feeling inspired and hit us with, "Fellas, let's go up there and start singing."

Even though all of us had nerve, that idea didn't go over too well.

Obie piped up, "No, man, this is New York. We can't be doing that here."

Lawrence persisted. "Damn it, we came here to hustle a job. We should just go up there and sing, it might turn into something. There's people here that can give us a break. They got shows to book, three or four acts a night."

We sat at the bar debating whether to go for it. Lawrence didn't quit. "Let's go up there and *sing*."

We finally agreed, since we knew he wasn't going to give up. "Okay, you're right, there might be some agents here."

We straightened our jackets, slicked back our hair, quickly commandeered the stage and took the mic. Surprisingly, it was still on. We started singing, "*Sometimes I'm happy, sometimes I'm blue…*" with no musical accompaniment, just a cappella, full harmony. We sounded just like The Four Freshmen. People stopped talking and started listening. We sang the whole song and nobody asked who the hell we were, told us to get us off the stage, or ran us out. People were clapping and calling out for more as we climbed off the stage.

And just like we had experienced at the Detroit Auto Show, a man materialized from the crowd, saying the words we wanted to hear. "Fellas, I'm an agent. I book a lot of the hotels up in the Catskills. You heard of 'em?"

It was a repeat of our Idlewild experience, except this time the resort was north of Manhattan, a summer retreat for New York Jews to enjoy time with their family in peace and tranquility among their own culture.

"Come to my office, let's talk. I might be able to book you all up there for a show." He handed me his card, making an appointment for the next morning. We showed up promptly, but his secretary was unexpectedly rude and condescending, making us wait until five or six o'clock before telling us he was too tied up to see us. But after waiting on him all day, we decided to keep sitting there until he left the office. He'd have no choice but see us on the way out and be forced to say something. When we didn't leave his secretary grew snippier. It probably infuriated her that we were acting as if we had minds of our own. As she started to insist that we leave immediately, the agent walked out of his office and he, too, seemed annoyed to see us there.

"Oh yeah, forgot you were here," he said, not apologetically.

That's how insignificant we were when we first started out. I attribute our staying power in the face of such disregard to the fact that there were four of us. It took our collective willpower to keep pushing against years of obstacles. And despite repeated discouragements and disappointments, there were people of every race and station in life who were helpful and kind from the moment we met them.

Such was the case with the owner of the Catskills resort, who invited us to join his family for lunch after knowing us for only ten minutes. About a week before, the rude agent called, arranging for an audition with this club owner. We sang just one song and he immediately hired us, insisting we sit down around a long picnic table, and treating us like we'd been a part of the family forever.

We were put up in a little five-bedroom shack on the grounds, which was all ours for the summer while we played several clubs in the Catskills area: the Pines, Flangers, and Klingers. Most of the entertainment was comprised of leading Black artists. On Saturday nights after the midnight show at the Pines, all the Black artists would get together and do a jam session. One night we wound up working with Cab Calloway, another night we jammed with Sarah Vaughan. Us four young guys just turning twenty were hanging with the greats. I felt bad that I had let down my mother not taking that college scholarship. However, the education I was getting as a young entertainer was priceless.

Slowly, word of mouth started spreading about The Four Tops' "all-American sound." We continued to hustle, never knowing where the next gig would lead. Criss-crossing the country, we picked up jobs at the Palm Springs Supper Club, and on the Playboy Penthouse circuit. We opened with Larry Steele's Smart Affairs, the largest Black entertainment touring group in the U.S. (also in Canada, Australia, and Puerto Rico) from the 40s through the 60s. We even scored a brief stint on Broadway in *Olivette Miller & Bert Gibson's Highlights*, a revue produced by the daughter of show business legend, Flournoy E. Miller. We were one degree of separation from the legendary Broadway lyricist, producer and playwright himself. Miller's Broadway show, *Shuffle Along*, had been the first all-Black musical on the Great White Way, a smash hit in the 20s. In Olivette's *Highlights*, the Tops performed big operatic numbers, successfully touring the Chitlin' Circuit en route to Broadway. We were singing alongside trained opera singers, holding our own and having a great time. To our dismay, the show only lasted four days in New York, but it only whet our appetite for more.

Daddy Braggs felt a growing paternal pride, noting how we were becoming more polished and professional each year. He felt we were ready to face one of the toughest audiences in the world. So without telling us he managed to get a booking at the famed Apollo Theater in Harlem, New York, where the audience was used to seeing only the best. If you didn't measure up, within minutes you'd be booed off the stage with no mercy.

When he shared this good news with us, we were stunned, wondering how he could have pulled this off without us having a hit record. "Don't you worry how I got the gig," he reassured us. "If y'all all sing like you do at my club they're going to love you. Plus, I'm going to have a surprise waiting for you when you get there. So go ahead of time, get with the band a day early. Then go to your rooms and check the surprise out."

Of course, when we got to New York we followed Daddy Braggs's direction to the letter. He met us as we checked into the rooming house he'd booked. Then he watched as we entered our rooms to find three suit boxes laid out on each bed. Inside were three of the most beautiful stage outfits that you could imagine. One was a brown Dupioni silk with matching pants, shoes, shirt, and tie. The second was a short Eisenhower-style waiter jacket made of maroon silk with black satin pants. And the third consisted of sparkling silver-grey jackets with contrasting black ties. We were absolutely speechless. Each outfit was more incredible than the next. We had a hard time deciding what to wear our first night.

We picked the silver jackets and had them on when we went down to rehearsal with the band. As we were warming up with songs from the American songbook rather than R&B, the bandleader, Ruben Philipps, realized that we weren't singing the Apollo's standard fare. With his musical ear, he could hear that our voices blended together in a four-part harmony that sounded like five. He whistled, thumbs up. "Boy, you guys can sing!" That helped with the show business jitters we were beginning to feel—after all, this was New York.

That night we opened with a song I'd made up, 'We're the Tops.' The lyrics went something like, "*We're the Tops, the places we'd like to go, the Sands in Las Vegas, Paris, Hollywood's the place for me, we're the Tops.*" After about four bars, the intimidating, hard-ass Apollo crowd started clapping. Then we sang 'In the Still of the Night,' a jazzy big band number that kind of soared in the air. I could feel the crowd's energy connecting with ours, catching the rhythm, popping their fingers, and nodding their heads. That's when it hit me: 'In the Still of the Night' was the song we were singing in my dream. The one I had after I told my mother I was going to become a singer and she begged me to pray to God for guidance. And here we were, just like in my dream, wearing the same amazing outfits, the silver jackets that flashed like stars under the lights. *My God it wasn't a dream, it was a sign, an affirmation.* Tears started coming from my eyes. The show was magnificent, ending with 'What I'd Say' by Ray Charles as we boogied off the stage. We got a standing ovation. It was just amazing. As soon as we got backstage, the guys saw me crying.

"Why the fuck you crying, Duke?"

"You remember my dream? These are same the outfits and we were singing 'In the Still of the Night.'"

That was another reminder that something bigger than us,

something we could not explain, had touched our lives. Once again, we hugged each other and recommitted to our dream. And to each other. *"No matter what… this was forever."*

* * *

Thanks to Daddy Braggs, we worked in the Idlewild Revue nearly every summer during the late 50s. After the summer season, he kept us busy in a travelling show in the fall and winter. He turned the Idlewild Revue into a touring show, booking noted artists like The Harlem Brothers; T-Bone Walker, a popular guitar player; Arthur Prysock, a handsome baritone jazz singer; even a dancer, Cliff Hurd, who could barely use his legs but danced his ass off on crutches. And of course, the dancing girls, the showgirls and The Four Tops. We had a lot of fun taking the show on the road. We worked in Chicago, Oklahoma, and quite a few other big cities. The last show we performed was in Boston in 1961, and three weeks into the tour the club caught fire and burned to the ground. All of our costumes, props, and everything else was destroyed. It totally broke Daddy Braggs's heart, as well as those of all of the entertainers he had nurtured over the years. It was like a family member had passed away. Daddy Braggs gathered himself together and said, "Well, folks, the show is over." Devastated, he went back to another of his passions, racing horses. He owned quite a few. Years later, in 1992, while watching one of his horses run in Virginia, Daddy Braggs had a fatal heart attack. It crushed us because he was more than just a producer. He was our *daddy*, our manager, a true visionary. He had the foresight to create the Idlewild Revue in the 50s, preceding Berry Gordy's Motortown Revue, while live performances were most popular, before the record business began to dominate. But Daddy Braggs was more than an entertainment impresario, he was a genuine father figure. Even today, when I think of him, he is sorely missed.

After our ties with Daddy Braggs ended, a new decade was upon us, and it seemed like a new era in music began. Things were changing in the entertainment industry. Berry Gordy was getting a foothold in the recording business, starting his own company in 1959. Billy Davis was going with Berry's sister, Gwen. Billy and Berry had remained close from their songwriting days. So it was only natural for Billy to begin working with Berry again. He approached us about making a deal. "Hey, you want to go with this company that Berry is starting?" he asked.

Our answer, which didn't take long for the four of us to agree on, was no. We hadn't been thrilled with what we'd heard about the two other Black-owned record companies that had recently started. Specifically, that they didn't treat their artists right, and that sales for these Black-owned companies were limited regionally. Also, we didn't want our music pigeon-holed into the solely R&B category. Berry's company didn't yet have a track record for selling nationally so we passed on the offer. Plus, we weren't actively pursuing a record deal then, and we felt that if we did we would look for a "real" record company. It didn't take long for us to realize we'd passed up a wonderful opportunity.

Meanwhile, Billy also chose another direction, deciding to focus on the advertising industry, writing jingles and slogans for radio and television commercials. He became vice president of McCann Erickson, one of the biggest advertising agencies in the world, writing and producing such identifiable and successful jingles as 'It's the Real Thing,' 'Things Go Better with Coke,' 'I'd Like to Buy the World a Coke,' for Coca-Cola, and 'If You've Got the Time We've Got the Beer,' for Miller High Life.

There were no hard feelings when we didn't jump at the chance to go with Motown. Billy also knew we saw our music and ourselves as more than just R&B, and that we wanted to go beyond that market. We weren't trying to be white and we weren't saying that we didn't like being Black. We were just saying that we were as good as anybody in the business, as any group, and wherever that led us that's where we were trying to go. Ironically, we learned later that was the same philosophy Berry Gordy laid out when he talked to his writers. He told them he didn't want them to write songs for just one corner of the world or just one neighborhood. He wanted them to write songs for everybody.'

Although we didn't sign with Motown, we kept working the R&B circuit. Jackie Wilson let us open his show while we were struggling between gigs. We got to see first-hand how crazy those one-night concerts could be for an R&B artist of his level. We saw the toll it took on Jackie, who missed a lot of shows, drinking and carrying on. We loved him, but we saw the kind of artist that we didn't want to be and the cost that compromising might exact from us. We had to figure out how to succeed on our own terms, singing our perfect harmonies and reaching out to a broader audience.

It was Twas at his Casablanca agency who got us one step closer to the kind of careers we were dreaming about. He'd started booking us at top-of-the-line nightclubs out West, inching us closer to big time venues in Las Vegas and Los Angeles. We started doing yearly appearances at the Eastwood Country Club in San Antonio, Texas, which was a big club with a casino in the back. Lots of Black G.I.s hung out there and gambled. There was an Air Force base nearby and other members of the armed forces were stationed in the area. In the audience one night, among all the uniforms and military crowd, was Major Riddle, one of the owners of the Dunes hotel and club in Vegas, a tall heavy-set guy with gang connections. When he approached us saying he wanted to book us to sing at the Dunes, our hearts skipped a beat. But there was one condition. He wanted us to bring our own rhythm section.

"How soon do you want us?" I said, not letting that large request stop us.

"How soon can you get it together?" he shot back.

Not wanting to waste another minute or let his enthusiasm wane, I threw out an answer, not thinking about how much time it would take to put together a group of musicians. One that could learn all of our material, rehearse, and travel across the country without much notice.

"Will you give us a couple of weeks?" I asked.

"I'll put you down for a date in two weeks."

As an afterthought I asked, "How much will you pay us?"
"How much do you charge?"

I just threw out a figure. I wasn't sure about Vegas bookings or how much to pay the band.

"What about sixteen hundred a week?"

"Okay, that's a deal."

I didn't know if this would cover all our expenses, travel, and accommodations, plus a salary, including our new rhythm section, but a deal was a deal.

We went back to Detroit and found four great musicians, guys we knew hanging in clubs and listening to music around the city: a pianist, Kirk Lightsey; a tenor player, Joe Henderson; a drummer, Roy Brooks; and a bass player whose last name was Cheryl. We rehearsed in Detroit for a couple of weeks and the four of us drove all the way to California in Levi's four-door Dodge without reverse. We sang all the way, rehearsing our material. At every stop we ran into segregation. When we got to Vegas we couldn't stay on the Strip. We stayed at a motel near what they called the Dust Bowl, which is where the Black entertainers lived, in the desert. But it didn't deter us. We didn't dwell on the fact that we were Black boys trying to make it in white clubs. We'd made it this far. We were young, bold, and full of confidence.

We opened with our rhythm section at the Dunes in 1959, calling ourselves The Four Tops + 4. I was in charge of payroll. We had to split sixteen hundred dollars a week among the eight of us, which didn't turn out to be that much. Two hundred dollars a piece, out of which we had to pay for our rooms and other expenses. Plus I had to send my earnings home to support my growing family. But being in Vegas was more important to me than making money. I probably would have paid to perform there. We were moving toward what we wanted to do. Unfortunately, I think I let our good luck get to my head.

Our first show started at four o'clock in the afternoon and our second was eight at night. In our down time between shows we started gambling. The last week of our gig I lost more money than I had, all of the + 4's payroll that was in my pocket. I kept on gambling thinking I would have a little winning streak, but it never happened. I lost it all. The reality of what I had just done hit me, and I was too embarrassed and panicked to tell anyone. I tried to figure out what I was going to do. I came up with a plan.

All of the wives of the Tops, except mine, had travelled to Las Vegas with us. Inez stayed home to take care of the kids. After the second show, I went to the cashier's window and got the rest of what was owed to us. It was just enough to pay the Tops, not the musicians. I went out the side door of the casino straight to Obie's wife, Val. I told her that I'd fucked up. I gave her the money to pay the Tops and quickly beat it to the airport. En route to Detroit I had a lay-over in Chicago. I decided to go Robert's Show Lounge, a club we'd worked in previously. Feeling sorry for my dumb ass, I sat at the bar drinking up what little money I had left. The club owner knew me and saw how upset I was. He felt sorry for me and the rest of the drinks were on the house. I sat there drinking and feeling terrible, but there was nothing I could do. It was like I'd just committed a hit and run. I couldn't even face my partners. When we finally talked about it back home, they didn't make a big deal about it; it was over and done with. I was relieved, but letting them down killed me.

I managed to get home and tried my best to forget what had happened, until I got a call from the Musicians' Union. The + 4 guys reported what I'd done. The union demanded that I make retribution. I agreed to do so, happy to pay fifty dollars out my forthcoming paychecks until I paid off the debt. Surprisingly, we remained friends. They all forgave me and I don't know how. I know I wouldn't have forgiven me. I probably would have kicked my own ass. After that I never in my life took another penny from anyone. It was a hard but important lesson, one that I will always regret learning the way I did. Never touch anyone else's money. Never use money for anything other than for what it was intended. But the even bigger lesson was I'd never do anything that would come between the Tops and me. I'd never again let that happen.

This lapse in my judgment created a terrible turning point in my marriage. The other wives had continued to dance up to that point, taking gigs, but Inez stopped to take care of Kai. It was hard on her financially with the group working only sporadically with lapses between paychecks. After she heard from the other wives what I'd done with the money in Vegas, she said, "…to hell with this." My poor judgment was too much for her. She asked me to leave. Sadly, I did, living in various places, hotels, with family members, a rented apartment, then finally a place of my own in a suburb outside of Detroit. The life I had chosen was difficult enough for me, but it was my dream. The toll it took upon my family was considerable. It was a sacrifice that I chose to make, and I couldn't expect my family to continue supporting my dreams indefinitely.

At this point the group had made enough headway for me to believe that realistically one day we'd be a success. We wouldn't have to worry about financial security. But we soon learned that that peace of mind was virtually non-existent in show business. It was something our next mentor, the legendary Billy Eckstine taught us. A velvety baritone, Eckstine was once the rival of Frank Sinatra. When he took us under his wing, he warned us, "…after the big parade, it gets quiet as a mouse. You have to be ready for that." So in-between gigs, we tried to keep busy and productive. We worked on our routine, rehearsed our music, and tried to hustle more gigs. We never knew how long these dry spells would last.

Being in the presence of great performers like "The Great Mr. B." helped sustain us. Billy schooled us from 1961 to 1963 when we sang back up for him. He was one of the best guys in the business. Not only was he handsome, he could sing his butt off too. Also, he was one of the sharpest dressers around. He had just recorded an album with The Hi-Lo's, a clean-cut white group renowned for their vocal harmonies. Someone told him that there were four Black guys who could sing four-part harmonies and may be able to go on the road with him. He invited us out to L.A. to audition. The week prior to our meeting, we learned four tunes from his album with The Hi-Lo's, and we had the numbers down by the time we flew out to L.A.

After greeting us in his apartment, Eckstine cut to the chase. "Well, now I've got to put you all through a test."

We responded with confidence, pointing to his recent LP. "Go ahead, which one of the songs do you want?"

"I don't want any of them songs," he said, handing us another recording. "I want you all to sing this one." Me, Obie, and Levi, were like, "*Shit, what're we gonna do?*"

Lawrence kept his cool. "Okay, let's hear it." Lawrence listened to the song, then asked Mr. B. to play it again. After hearing it twice, he requested, "Can we go in the bathroom for five minutes?"

Mr. B. was cool. "Sure, take your time, motherfucker."

In the bathroom, Lawrence taught us the first verse and chorus of the song. Ten minutes was all it took for us to learn those parts. We had developed an ear by then from working with Lawrence, and we could pick up a four-part close harmony almost as well as he could, though Lawrence always could hear it first. After our quick rehearsal, we were confident and prepared to go back out and tell Mr. B. we were ready. He nodded, still real nonchalant, "Sing, motherfuckers, go ahead."

We started singing, really getting into it, and he abruptly broke in. "Hold it right there. I tell you what, I can pay y'all eight hundred dollars a week. Y'all are some singing motherfuckers, baby!"

Mr. B. was impressed by our vocal ability. He was less enthusiastic about our energetic dance moves. While we were performing, singing back up for him, we were having such a ball we must have gotten carried away. Prancing around, doing so many dance steps that by the end of the songs, we were singing flat. Mr. B. wouldn't stand for that. "I hired y'all to sing, not to be dancing around my fucking stage. Cut out them goddamn steps. That's one thing I can't have is nobody singing flat on my stage." That's the way he talked, a mixture of gangsta' bluntness and hard-core showbiz profanity. He didn't mince his words. We quickly got the message. Billy was a real pro. We knew we were lucky to hang around him and soak up his knowledge. We had been groomed by show business professionals, promoters, booking agents, record executives, and managers, but we had never been schooled by a legendary singer. We studied the way Mr. B. dressed, the way he gambled, his proficiency on the golf course, his vocal delivery, and the finesse he had with his fans. We benefited from everything he taught us. Especially the wisdom he laid on us about careers slowing down after reaching peaks and crescendos. After we wrapped up our gig with him, we got a tip from a promoter friend who turned us on to a recording company in New York. We were lucky enough to immediately sign another recording contract.

Our deal with Riverside Records was for four songs. The stipulation was that if one of them became a hit, they would give us a full record deal. While we were in the studio, the success of Motown Records became the topic of conversation. Everyone had been following the amazing impact this upstart company had been having on the industry with at least two or three hit records constantly on the charts. We had already been through two or three other record deals by then, and we asked ourselves why we were recording in New York instead of back in Detroit with Motown. We agreed that it sure would be nice to have a deal back home.

In the meantime, since we were in the vicinity, we picked up a few gigs in the Catskills. One night a talent scout from the *Tonight Show* was in the audience. Afterwards, he approached us.

"I'd love to have you guys perform that number, 'In the Still of the Night,' on my show," he said.

"When?" It didn't take more than the blink of an eye for me to try to seal the deal.

"As soon as you can," he responded. "How long you gonna be in the area?"

After a brief conversation, we settled on a date for the following week when we'd be back in the City.

The other date we were excited about was seeing the Motown Revue at the Apollo Theater. At that time Motown had only been around for two or three years so the Revue wasn't what it eventually grew to be. Still, The Marvelettes had already scored a hit. Martha and the Vandellas had a hit. Mary Wells and Marvin Gaye were also on the bill. Watching the show that night, we were so impressed that someone would package a show with young Detroit artists and put them in the spotlight. We kept looking at each other, wishing we were in it. We knew we would tear it up. Also, we regretted not signing with Motown when we had had the chance. But we had faith that whatever happened in our careers, it would be for the best. We had faith in something greater than us having a hand in our lives. And once again, elements conspired to lift our voices higher and closer to reaching the audience we had been aiming for.

While we were singing on the *Tonight Show* in New York, Berry Gordy was watching TV in Detroit with his director of A&R, William "Mickey" Stevenson.

"Damn man," Berry had said to him. "I always liked the Tops. I love them singing those old standards. I don't have nobody in my stable like that. Do you know how to get in touch with them?"

"Yeah," Mickey told him, "…we're great pals."

We were in New York just finishing up our Riverside recording when Mickey reached us. Both Obie and I had known Mickey as a successful songwriter, producer, and the man who had organized Motown's legendary in-house band, The Funk Brothers. Now he was doing artist development. We were amazed when he told us, "Man, Berry wants you all. Sounds like he wants y'all bad."

Later, we learned he had been following our career. He described his impression of us: "Smooth, classy, and polished; they were big stuff. I could see how loyal they were to each other, and I knew they would be the same way to me and Motown."

Just as excited as he was about us, we eagerly finished our recording and went straight to Detroit. Two days later, we drove over to Hitsville, an ordinary looking house on West Grand Boulevard (a few blocks down from the General Motors headquarters), which Berry Gordy had transformed into his mega recording company. Up in Berry's office, he gave us a wonderful greeting.

"Man, I love you guys. I remember seeing you all at the Flame Show Bar and other places around town. I love the way y'all sing, especially the old standards. Those wonderful jazz sounds, beautiful harmonies."

It was music to our ears. We were holding our breath, until we heard him say: "How would you like to join Motown?"

"Man, that would be great." I spoke for all of us, knowing it was what we'd been hoping and praying for. "And it's actually ironic, because we were hoping we could find some type of way to join Motown."

He laughed. "Well, maybe this is the time."

We explained how easy it was for us to learn songs, that we liked all kinds of music, but that we wanted to go further than just the R&B circuit. We believed The Four Tops were bigger than that.

Berry agreed, saying that he didn't want any of his artists stuck into that little corner.

"So I'd like to offer you all a deal," he said pulling out a contract and passing it across his desk. "Here's one of my contracts. It's for six years. Look it over and tell me what you want." It was obvious he meant, look it over right now while we were sitting there.

I paused, having gained six years of experience acting as the Tops' unofficial spokesperson, handling most of the business.

"Well, what we'd like to do, Berry," I said knowing that the Tops would back me up, "'is take the contract home and study it a little bit.'"

He pushed back. "Oh no," he said, "I never let my contracts out of my office. I don't do that."

I was pretty confident in negotiating, so I said, "Berry, you know that we've signed a couple of record deals, but we always have to look it through and see what's in it. It's business, you know." I could tell he wasn't used to this kind of exchange with his artists.

"Well, I do business different ways," he said. "You sign it right here or not."

I stood my ground. I was accustomed to listening to Mr. B. and Daddy Braggs, even my own Daddy who spoke up for his rights as an Indian immigrant. I guess that's where I got the courage to say, "Well, man, we can't just sign it sight unseen. As much as we'd love to be here, we're gonna have to take it home and look at it, you know."

I guess he could tell we weren't going to back down.

"Well, you need your attorney to look at it?" he asked.

"Maybe, but maybe we can read it," I said, now understanding what his main concern was.

"We're going to read it ourselves, and talk it through overnight." I assured him.

He thought about it a minute; he cussed a little, almost angry. "Okay, man. I don't usually do this kind of shit. You can bring it back tomorrow."

So we left, sat around, and studied the contract. It appeared to be a standard contract. We reviewed the basic things, read the top of each paragraph, and understood most of it. We saw a provision to use us as background singers on certain records for which we would be compensated a small fee of six dollars and a twenty-five cents as a voice for hire with no royalties. This didn't pose a problem since we had sung back up for other artists in the past for a small cut of the royalties, but the records never sold, so it didn't matter. All we were looking for was getting our own hits from the company. What concerned us most was that there was no mention of an advance upon signing, which was something we needed and had to address.

As we kept talking trying to figure it all out, Levi shook his head growing frustrated. "Look at all this paper. It takes an attorney to read a contract. I don't really want to be involved with all this. This is *Motown*. What are we gonna do?"

Obie and Lawrence were also tired of trying to figure it out. They chimed in, "We've been to Columbia Records, Chess, Riverside. And we still don't have a hit."

They were right. I sat staring at the contract, unsure of what our next move should be.

"What the fuck, man? This is home," Levi said helping me out. "Gordy's making hits. This seems like where we ought to be."

There was really nothing more to talk about. We all agreed: we'd go for it.

The next day we were back in Berry's office ready to sign the contract if he would give us an advance.

"Look, man, I don't do that," he said after hearing what we needed to sign. "But here's what I'll do, I guarantee that you'll have hits at this record company. Y'all are good enough, I know

I can make you hits."

"Can you put it in writing?" I asked.

"No. But I can guarantee you'll have hits," he said.

"Since you know we'll have hits," I said, knowing this was a strong possibility, "we're just asking for an advance against the money you'll be making."

He thought about this for a minute and then reached into his pocket. "Look, here's the best I can do. I got four hundred dollars. One hundred dollars for each of you." He laid the money on the table.

We looked at each other. This wasn't what we expected—we wanted more, we needed more—but it was something. It was Motown, and we were on our way.

❧ 5 ❧

The Road To The Top

E very artist had a different relationship with Berry Gordy. Some people were mad at him about early royalties. But my relationship with him was always positive, and over the years I learned he would match what you put into the relationship. The Tops were already established before he signed us. He didn't discover four young R&B singers, break them in and groom them like he did with so many others. He recognized that we were a popular, well-regarded group before we got there. We already had a distinct sound and musical identity. He never stated an intention to reshape us. And from the start, he said he wanted to release an album of us singing jazz standards on his label. We couldn't have been happier.

Berry's vision was that Mickey Stevenson would produce our initial American songbook LP for a new jazz label he was starting. Since the Tops had been doing their thing for so long, Berry told us to pick whoever we wanted to write our arrangements, the size of our band, how many horn players we needed, and whether we wanted a rhythm section or just a combo. He left the creative decisions up to us. We were excited to get this kind of artistic respect and freedom. We told Mickey that we wanted a live recording with big band arrangements. We picked Ernie Wilkins, who wrote for Count Basie, and Gil Askey, who had written for us in Atlantic City, to do the arrangements. They both agreed to come to Motown and work with the four of us. Once they arrived, we all sat down with Mickey and picked the songs, which we started learning right away while the arrangements were being written.

The first day we recorded a live session with everyone— musicians and artists, the horns, the rhythm section, and the vocals—all in one room. It wasn't like it is now, where if you make a mistake you can stop, rewind, and re-record. Back in 1963, it had to be done in one take all the way through. As we recorded, we made a couple of mistakes, and the band made some too. We were only able to get through one whole song that first day, although three had been scheduled. Nevertheless, it was a remarkable session because it was the first time Motown had ever done anything live in their studios, all the musicians and singers all together in a room recording at the same time. It took us about three months to successfully record twelve songs with that big band. Then it was decided we would record eight more with a smaller band at the Graystone Ballroom, a historic downtown landmark where greats like Ella Fitzgerald, Duke Ellington, and Glenn Miller had played. Berry had purchased it in 1963 and installed a new sound system so that Motown's acts could perform in a magnificent venue.

We turned the Graystone into a recording studio for a live audience. Berry put out word that The Four Tops would be appearing at the Graystone for a one-night concert. We had a full house, and played an amazing repertoire of jazz standards, and even one blues tune, 'Every Day I Have the Blues,' once recorded by Joe Williams and also Memphis Slim. Back then it took about five months to mix the album and complete it with all the finishing touches. We couldn't wait to hear the finished product. We were so proud and excited that we had finally accomplished our goal. *Breaking Through* was the album we had dreamed of, an LP of American standards, with tunes like 'I Left My Heart in San Francisco,' 'Fascinating Rhythm,' and 'I Could Have Danced All Night,' from the Broadway musical *My Fair Lady*. Little did we know as we walked into Berry's office to hear it for the first time, it wouldn't be released for over thirty-five years.

Berry ushered us into the office with Mickey Stevenson and after we listened to a few cuts, he broke the news that he didn't think it was the right direction for us to go in.

"Good sound, great sound, man," he said, as he stopped the recording. "This is all good stuff, but I want you to hear what these three young writers are doing in this office over here." He motioned to one of his adjoining buildings. He kept talking, putting our dreams for *Breaking Through* on hold and shifting gears. "I'm going to put this out eventually, but to be honest it's just not commercial enough." We didn't say anything; we didn't know what to think given how much he and everyone else involved had invested in it emotionally and creatively.

"I want y'all to go over there and meet them, Eddie Holland, Brian Holland, and Lamont Dozier. They call themselves Holland–Dozier–Holland."

"We know them, just not that well," I said. "Eddie Holland's a great singer, he sounds just like Jackie Wilson."

Berry laughed. "That's the thing, he thinks he's a better writer than singer. Go over with Mickey and he'll introduce you. I'll call over there and tell them we need them to write you some hits."

That's how it started with HDH. Mickey made the official introductions, but we recognized each other from years of running into each other around town. They complimented our singing, then relayed Berry's message to them. He wanted "hit songs."

"Well, y'all got a little hit out with Martha, 'Come and Get These Memories,'" I said. "And it looks like you're going to have a hit with the Supremes." We'd heard a few of their cuts in the making.

Lamont nodded, smiling graciously. "Yeah, we got a little thing going, but we'd love to work with y'all."

More than a musical collaboration began that day: it was a friendship. The Four Tops' new musical direction couldn't have been in better hands. We were somewhat disappointed when Berry revealed that he had another vision for us, beyond jazz standards. Even though we were doubtful, we trusted him. It paid off, big-time.

While HDH were busy working on material, we kept busy singing background vocals for other Motown artists. We were booked almost every night with either Martha and the Vandellas, Marvin Gaye, The Marvelettes, or Kim Weston. Many of our back-up vocals didn't make the records, but we were averaging two sessions a night. It all added up to Thursday night paychecks of about $37.50, sometimes as little as $20.50.

We were no longer touring and traveling on the road, so that amounted to little more than pocket money, nothing to get excited about. But what did excite us while singing back-up was learning how to record in the studio, how to put feeling into our singing with no audience to feed off, and how to get the nuances of our sound right. We impressed everyone by how quickly we could knock out background vocals. Motown had a female session group, The Andantes, three fabulous singers who did back-up for Martha and the Vandellas, The Temptations, The Supremes, The Marvelettes, and others. Folks started calling us the male Andantes. Word soon spread and everyone wanted us to sing background for them, which we did for a couple of months until things started clicking.

As the new additions to Motown's family, we started hanging around Hitsville even when we weren't working. We were having the time of our life because we were making great friends with everybody, The Temptations, The Miracles, The Supremes. Little Stevie Wonder was this cute young man, like a kid in a toyshop. He played all kinds of instruments. If a studio was empty, he would go in and beat on the drums, then play the piano, making music with whatever he could find. If we were sitting in the reception area, we'd see people coming and going, and we could hear music coming from all the studios. It was like our own little campus students' union, that's how close we were getting. Most of the artists were young, seventeen or eighteen, and we were just a little older. Motown was like a college of music. It was an exciting time.

While we were waiting for HDH to write us one of their

masterpieces, we landed a gig at the 20 Grand, one of Detroit's most prestigious nightclubs, a very classy place where all the top acts performed. We were good friends with the owner, Bill Kabbus, who learned we were back in town. He told us we could work there whenever we wanted. We had just wrapped a show at his club one night, when Brian Holland showed up in our dressing room.

"Fellas, I got the song," he announced. "I got y'a'll a hit!"

"Yeah?" We got all excited. "What's the song?"

"I got it on tape," he said, playing it on his cassette. He sang along with just a piano accompanying. "It's called 'Baby I Need Your Loving,'" he said, apparently hearing it in his head in all its glory. All we could hear were the bare bones.

"Well, it sounds okay. What are you going to put with it?" I asked.

"We got a little rhythm track cut in the studio already. I just wanted to bring you the song to see if you like it."

"Yeah, we like it," we said, feeding more off his excitement than what we could hear on tape.

"Will you come to the studio and record it?" he asked, really stoked about his new song.

We looked at each other, silently communicating. *"Now?"* *"Well, why not?"* *"Let's go with it."*

"Yeah, are you kidding? Yeah!" one of us answered. We were still pumped from our 20 Grand performance. "We're in good voice and shit, we're ready."

So off we went to the studio at two thirty in the morning to record our first HDH tune for Motown.

Toasting the success of 'Baby I Need Your Loving' with Berry Gordy and HDH.
MOTOWN ARCHIVES/AVALON

Hitsville in the middle of the night was humming with other artists doing their own thing and checking out what else was going on. Brian wanted us to work on backgrounds first with Eddie Kendricks singing the melody so we could hear it, while he talked us through how the background vocals should go. Lamont joined in helping explain the background and the kind of vocal arrangement they wanted, which Lawrence quickly picked up on. HDH broke down the harmonies they heard each of us singing. Then we jumped right in and after a few tries Lamont said, "Oh man, that's great. Let's go on ahead and record it, y'all ready?"

Things were moving pretty fast. I nodded saying, "Well, we need to iron out a few wrinkles, but we're about ready."

In the studio, we sang the backgrounds for about ten minutes before they told Levi to go work with Eddie on the melody. While we were still recording in the booth, we watched Eddie and Levi really hitting it off, getting into the vocals, discussing things as they went along. That was a great sign. After about twenty minutes, the HDH guys were happy with the background recordings, and said we were done. But we were so used to doing background for other artists, we asked if we could do one more for safety's sake. We always liked to do an extra take at the end because once we nailed it, we learned if we did it again, the next one might be better. Either way you can't lose. And actually, the last one turned out even stronger.

Eddie, Brian, and Lamont were more than happy. "Oh man, this is fabulous. Now that you're through, want to listen to Levi and Eddie test out the lead?"

"Oh, yeah." We were loving every minute so far.

Checking out Levi and Eddie working on the melody, we noticed that the lyrics to 'Baby I Need Your Loving' were already printed out. But Levi had a pen and pad and was writing the words again on a separate piece of paper.

"Lee, why are you doing that?" I asked him. "The words are already right there."

"I have to write them to feel them," he said. He did that with every song. He'd write out the lyrics even if they had been printed out for him before. After he wrote them himself, Levi sang it through with Eddie a couple of times, listening to each other, trading ideas, and collaborating to come up with the best delivery and vocalization. Levi then went into the booth and in just three takes he nailed it. And that was it, we had just finished our first HDH recording. We had been in the studio for a little over an hour. As we left Hitsville that night, we overheard them saying, "These motherfuckers can sang. These cats can really sing!" 'Baby I Need Your Loving' turned out to be the easiest recording we ever made, proof to us that our destiny with Motown was "signed, sealed and delivered!" as Stevie Wonder put so well.

* * *

The Tops had been away from Detroit for so long, I was now separated from my wife, and neither Lawrence nor I had a place to stay. The day we signed our contract, Janie Bradford, a Motown songwriter, overheard me saying I was going to get a room in a hotel. After being a married man, I didn't want to move back home with my mom. Janie offered to rent the two of us her private guest quarters. She had a big beautiful house with private quarters in the back. It was weird staying in a hotel in my hometown, so Lawrence and I gratefully accepted.

However we spent most of our time at Motown anyway, hanging around the studio with The Supremes. By then we were like their big brothers. They were sweet, skinny little seventeen-year-old girls. When we weren't at Hitsville we would go over to Mary Wilson's house in the Brewster Projects to party. We'd drink beer and wine mixed together, which we called sluice. They didn't have a hit yet, and we didn't either, but we liked the way they sang, we loved the way they looked, and we were all working round the clock trying to get a hit.

About a week after our late-night recording session with HDH, we were at Motown sitting outside the studio in the reception area with The Supremes and The Temptations when I thought I heard 'Baby I Need Your Loving' playing in the distance. "Hold up," I said. "Wait a minute, that's our song. You hear it?"

Obie and I jumped up and ran over to the studio, listening to the tune, now with strings from the Detroit Symphony orchestra, Funk Brothers' horns, and The Andantes' background vocals. It was so big and full it sounded like a whole chorus backing us up.

"God damn, that shit is big! It sounds beautiful, man."

We were thrilled, thinking our record was about to be released, but it would take months to happen. In the meantime, The Supremes' singles 'Where Did Our Love Go' and 'Baby Love' came out. They were both number one smash hits, of course written by HDH, who were unstoppable at this point. The Supremes followed with another HDH hit, 'Come See About Me,' which was climbing the charts fast. It was at that point that Berry released our first Motown recording in 1964, without us even knowing it.

It had taken so long, the Tops weren't together when this greatly anticipated moment happened. Obie was in Atlantic

City watching his wife dance with the Larry Steele Dancers. The rest of us were in Detroit. I'd just left Hitsville and was on my way home when I heard it on the car radio. This was before FM radio and there were no regular R&B stations. 'Baby I Need Your Loving' was playing on WJBK and hearing it out of the blue blew me away.

"Man, that sounds like a hit!" I said to my buddy, who was driving me around because I still didn't have a car. I knew my luck was changing fast. "Take me back to the studio."

I went straight in to speak to HDH, who said they were getting a great response already. I immediately called Levi, and he'd just heard it on the radio. We got in touch with Obie who was excited that it had been played on a Philadelphia station, too. Finally, we were able to track down Lawrence who came to the studio, where HDH played it for him. With his musical ear, he marveled at the production, recalling how raw the song had been to start with and how beautiful it now was with the strings, background vocals, equalizing and other technical enhancements. We were so confident that we had a hit on our hands, we knew we'd better start rehearsing a new show right away.

We weren't wrong. 'Baby I Need Your Loving' was climbing the charts, and we immediately got a booking at the Phelps Lounge, a cool club with a sexy curved bar on Oakland Avenue. Now was the perfect time to buy new uniforms but we were hard up for cash. Obie agreed to loan the group some money from the stash he always kept. He got his sister to throw in a little bit more. She agreed that since we were coming out with something new, we should have new outfits too. We headed back down to our old buddy at Hot Sam's and bought nice brown sport jackets and pants to match.

I was feeling pretty good about the future when my mother called. I was hesitant about what she'd say about 'Baby I Need Your Loving.' I knew she was still upset with me about singing these kinds of unreligious songs. It caught me off guard when she started by asking if I was working somewhere in town. The people she cleaned for had inquired if she knew a group called The Four Tops. She admitted that her son was in it. They were excited about our song on the radio and they wanted to see us perform. Proudly, I told her about our gig at the Phelps Lounge and for a minute it felt good that I could not only help them get tickets but that we were the stars of the show. But the more I thought about it, the more it didn't feel right. My mother was a maid, scrubbing white folks' floors, cleaning their toilets, and changing their sheets. They were paying her next to nothing. Now they were asking her to help them get tickets to hear her son sing. I called her back.

"Let me tell you something, Mama," I said. "I don't like the idea of this whole thing, especially you working for these folks."

"I got to work somewhere, son," she said.

"No, you don't. I'm going to a find a way to retire you," I said, with a confidence that just kept growing. "That ain't all, you go find yourself a house. Somewhere to live other than the apartment that you stay in."

"You don't have to do that," she said, cautiously.

"We're going to have some hit records," I told her. "I think I might make some real money, Mama."

"Well, I sure hope so," she said. "Because believe it or not, me and your sister are just barely making it off what's left of her child support each month. But we've been looking for a house. One that's not too expensive, but big enough for me, the girls and all the kids. I think we found one."

"Go check it out," I said, not knowing where I was going to get the money but determined to figure it out. At this time in my life I was very young and very aggressive. I did crazy stuff that I knew I wasn't supposed to do. Somehow luck was always with me. I had the kind of bravery my daddy must have had jumping into the Detroit River. One time I even rented a car without a license, and kept it for a year! When the rental company finally caught up with me, I told them somebody stole it. I had actually given it to the girl I was going with. But after my + 4 experience, I was just as wild but also a lot wiser. I knew I was no longer going to break the law. And I knew I had to find the money to buy my mother a house, whatever it took.

A week before our Phelps Lounge engagement, my mama called to tell me that she'd found the house she wanted. Now I had to deliver. The only thing I could think of was to ask Berry Gordy. At that time I thought I was a smart cookie, that I could talk and reason with anyone, regardless of who they were. Berry was my boss, only about two or three years older than me. I felt we had developed a kind of friendship. We had played poker a few times together. I knew that family and loyalty were important to him too. Motown was really like an extended family.

I also knew Berry was a betting man. He liked to gamble. It wasn't part of his professional image, but in private he let his guard down. There was one time I was at Mary Wilson's house hanging out, and Berry stopped by to pick her up for a television appearance. While Mary went upstairs to finish getting dressed, Berry and I had a drink. Berry suggested that we finish up a card game we'd started a couple nights before. I still owed him two hundred dollars. Berry suggested we play blackjack. I got the cards and dealt him a hand for the two hundred. I won that hand, and we were even. He said we should play another hand for two hundred, which I also won. Then he doubled it for four hundred. I won again. The next hand we played for eight hundred. I won. Berry kept doubling the stakes. So we played for sixteen hundred. Believe it or not, I blackjacked that hand.

"You a lucky motherfucker, man," he said, doubling it again.

Now we were playing for thirty two hundred dollars. I won. I guessed by then that he was ready to fold.

"Wait a minute, I ain't through," he said. "Let's make up the difference, ten thousand dollars or nothing. If you win, I'll owe you ten. And you ain't going to owe me nothing."

I swear on the Bible, I blackjacked that hand.

"Mr. B." I said, gleefully, "you know, you owe me ten thousand dollars."

"Well, come to my office tomorrow," he said, and that was it.

The next day I showed up and he paid me the ten thousand, plus another check for twenty-five hundred to pay the taxes on it. It was like he didn't think nothing of it, not mad or nothing.

Knowing that Berry would sometimes take risks, and hoping he'd bet on me paying him back, I headed over to Hitsville and went straight up to Berry's office. I knew I'd have to talk to his personal secretary, who sat outside the door. Of course, she asked if I had an appointment. When I said I did not, I tried to impress upon her that this was really important. She told me that I had to make an appointment first, I just couldn't walk in and see him. So I sat down in front of her and started talking and sure enough we discovered that we were born on the same day in the same year. She just couldn't believe it. After that she started warming up to me and after about an hour, she said Berry must be finishing up his meeting soon. She picked up the phone and buzzed him.

I could hear the other side of the conversation as she said one of The Four Tops wanted to see him. He asked her what it was about. She said that she didn't know, but it sounded important. He told her he'd be done in ten minutes; he'd see me then. Soon afterwards Berry came out of his office deep in conversation with Barney Ales, his head of Sales and Promotion. I overheard them talking about a group in England doing a cover of a Supremes tune, and Motown needed to figure out a way to prevent them from releasing their record before Motown's. Barney assured Berry not to worry—he'd get to the bottom of things and take care of it.

Young Barney Ales was like a Mafia guy; he wasn't actually in the mob but that's the way he sold records. He was more than close to Berry and crucial to Motown's success. He knew how to deal with distributors and buyers, get them to take Motown product and make sure they sold it. He was a mastermind of selling Black records in the segregated South and set the precedent. Part of Berry's genius was that he always surrounded himself with the right people.

I was intrigued about how Barney operated. I had an old friend from middle school, Irving Biegel, who worked in Motown's sales and promotion department. I asked if I could hang with him to see how things worked. While I was there someone called to order twenty thousand Supremes records. Barney told Irving how to handle it: "Here's what you got to do. Say we'll send you forty thousand, no returns. We'll ship them to you, don't send nothing back. Bye." That's the way Barney did business. Motown believed in what they were selling; they didn't worry about forcing more records on people, because they knew they'd sell. No one would ask to send anything back. Of course all of the records that were shipped sold. Barney's high-pressure tactics probably had as much to do with Motown's early growth as anything else.

So after Barney departed, Berry invited me in his office, complimenting me on how well our record was doing. He had no idea I was about to use that as a bargaining chip to ask for an advance.

"Look, Berry," I said. "I got a small problem, but it shouldn't be that big to you. I need you to loan me some money."

He cut me off. "Man, I don't do this."

I kept going. "Look, my mama's scrubbing these white people's floors and she needs a house. I remember you guaranteeing us hits. I know we going to have another hit after this one. So I'm just asking would you please loan me ten thousand dollars?"

He said, "Duke, I don't usually loan artists that kind of money."

"Well, just advance me the money, man," I said. Then I told him about the lady my mama worked for who wanted to come hear The Four Tops sing. "That's a bunch of shit to me. I need to buy her a house so she can stop scrubbing these folks' floors. You got to help me get my mama off her fucking knees. I don't know no other way."

He started laughing and said, "Duke, let me think about it. Come back tomorrow."

I was so relieved on my way out I thanked the secretary and told her almost the whole story. She reassured me that if Berry told me to come back it was a good sign. "When he says no, that's it. There ain't no coming back."

Feeling hopeful I returned the next day and not one check awaited me, but two. One for ten thousand dollars and another for twenty-five hundred for the taxes. I almost cried. I told Berry that he had just saved my mama and I was so grateful I would never let him down. I couldn't express it in words.

Berry simply said, "Man, go on and do what you got to do."

Check in hand, I went straight to my mama's and told her I had the money. She was as surprised as I was. And since I didn't have a car, we found ourselves a ride and went over to the house on Orangelawn Street. It really was a nice house. The total cost was fifteen thousand. I gave her four thousand five hundred for a down payment and promised that I'd keep up the monthly payments.

"Oh baby, you can do that, son?" she asked.

"I don't know, Mama, but I'm sure gonna try. If it's up to me you won't have to work another day in your life."

She sat there and cried. I did too.

With the rest of the money I went downtown and bought four pairs of alligator shoes. And I put a down payment on a Cadillac. Then I hung out that whole weekend crying from one bar to the next, getting high and sobbing I was so happy. I didn't know I could be that happy.

A few days after my mama moved in, my whole family went over to the house to celebrate. The first thing Mama did was bless the house. By that time she was a minister, but back when she was the church piano player and then the choir director, she was always encouraging me to sing and always believing in me. That day she was as happy as I've ever seen her, and so were my sister and her little kids. It was just a joy. I remember thinking, *"Lord, you can take me right now with a smile on my face."*

I had taken care of my mother. I was doing the best I could to help my father too. I was so proud that I had taken the first steps a son should to help his parents. I knew they had given me all that they could. Not monetary stuff, but they instilled wonderful things in me that came out in my dealings with people. The way I tried to talk to people. The way I conducted myself in public. The way people responded to me. I know I learned it all from those two. Probably from my grandmother too. I've always felt so blessed. I don't think I've ever experienced another more blessed moment than that weekend.

* * *

Berry did more than just sell records. He plucked his young protégés from the streets of Detroit and turned them into stars. It was similar to the Hollywood Studio System in the 30s and 40s when talented young actors were made to look like American royalty. Berry came up with a division called Artist Development. In a building across the street from the studio, Maxine Powell ran a successful Modeling and Finishing School. She gave instruction to The Supremes and others on how to conduct themselves like ladies. Classes were taught in etiquette, speaking correctly, how to dress, eat, and give interviews in public. Miss Powell was so successful that when The Supremes and The Beatles (who were big Motown fans) first met in England, The Beatles were let down. The Supremes were all dressed up and acting lady-like, and The Beatles, who were from working-class Liverpool, thought The Supremes were uptight and over-dressed. They expected them to let their hair down and have a raucous good time. But that's not the image that Berry wanted them to project. Their new, classy, upgraded look made them into one of the biggest acts in show business.

Motown's Artist Development also included classes with the famed dancer Cholly Atkins, who had been part of a legendary vaudeville dance act, Atkins and Coles. They appeared at the Apollo, toured with jazz greats like Louis Armstrong and even appeared on Broadway in *Gentlemen Prefer Blondes*. Cholly was good at coming up with choreography for different musical arrangements teaching each act a unique routine. He was so integral to Berry's assembly line that as soon as an act had a record coming out, they were sent to Artist Development . Someone had already written their music, given them great arrangements for the stage, provided amazing costumes, now the artist needed help perfecting their live performance. Most of these kids had never been on the road before and in order to be a success it took more than just recording in the studio. Cholly taught them how to enhance their vocal performances with dance moves, hand gestures, and what it took to have a great stage presence.

By the time The Four Tops got to Motown we had already perfected our stage presentation. We knew how to come up with dance moves for specific arrangements. In fact, Gil Askey, one of the arrangers we brought to Motown for our first album, was so expert at putting together live acts that Berry hired him to be the conductor for The Supremes. From then on, he arranged all of their shows, handling everything for them musically. So even though the Tops were experienced live performers they still scheduled us once every three months to brush up with Cholly. He used to laughingly call us The Renegades. Each session was supposed to cover just one song, but we would take five or six steps across the boards and be finished with all five. We listened to Cholly's ideas, but unlike the Temps, we kept our dancing to a cool minimum, always remembering what Billy Eckstine told us when we danced ourselves out of breath and started singing flat.

The reaction we were getting from just one hit record was amazing. Right away Motown wanted us to start working on another song, 'Ask the Lonely.' Soon we discovered that big money didn't automatically come with hit records. It would be two years before we cleared a royalty check. In order to make a living we started gigging again. Part of Motown's package was their management company, the International Talent Management Inc (ITMI), run by Esther Gordy, Berry's sister. We jokingly called it 'shit me.' When they put on the Motown Revue, the Motown management company would buy each act for twelve days, and give us x amount of dollars, and take out their percentages for management. I don't know how much they made, though I'm sure it was a lot. But the artists were satisfied with the deals made by the company and in the beginning nobody was really concerned about a conflict of interest. Later some of us found other representation: Stevie went with Ewart Abner, Smokey worked with Suzanne dePasse, and we eventually went with Ron Strassman.

Esther was a tough negotiator, though. She made good deals for everybody. Our deal to appear in the Revue for ten days amounted to the Tops making about eighty thousand dollars. I can't remember the exact figures, but if there were six other acts, they were given similar deals. After a couple of years, the price to package all of the artists went sky high, since everyone's success kept growing. Ultimately, they couldn't afford to put a

Revue together. Being in the Motown Revue was one of the first gigs we had after joining the company. It was a joy performing onstage and thinking back to when we had been applauding the Revue sitting in the Apollo audience. Just a year earlier, we'd pictured how we would tear it up if we had the chance.

Our reputation was spreading with the success of our first ballad, 'Ask the Lonely,' which we thought was strong and beautiful, especially Levi's delivery. Esther approached us with a "remote" offer from the West Coast to appear in a show with Count Basie. It was just for a couple of dates, but the money was pretty good and she would ask for a deposit so we'd have enough to get out there. It sounded good to us. We were big Count Basie fans harkening back to the day when we took over the mic in between his sessions in New York. Esther got everything down in a contract and we flew to L.A. where a young guy met us at the airport, an aspiring concert promoter named Dick Griffey.

When we got to L.A., Dick Griffey started off by telling us that the date didn't look good. In fact, he didn't even think Count Basie was going to come. He asked if we would accompany him to the venue to check on ticket sales to see if he could salvage it. When we got there the ticket sales were virtually nil. We felt bad for Dick and tried to let him off the hook, because we saw what this ambitious young brother was trying to do, and we appreciated him putting us on the bill with Basie. We told him that he could cancel if he wanted to and we wouldn't charge him a penalty, even though there were provisions in our contract to protect us. Seeing how disappointed and embarrassed he was, since evidently he hadn't advertised enough, we wound up telling him that he'd get it right one day and we'd work together down the line. He was so grateful, and because we were booked to stay for a few more days he had another bright idea.

"What I can do is show y'all a nice party," he said. "I know this cat that owns a club down on Crenshaw. You can go down there and hang out."

So instead of performing with Count Basie we wound up having a few drinks, smoking and doing a couple of other little things that they did in California at that time, all the time building Dick Griffey back up. The next time it would work out, we reassured him. Eventually he proved us right. Griffey went on to found Soul Train Records with Don Cornelius and his own label, Solar (Sound of Los Angeles Records), which had a major impact on R&B in the 70s and 80s.

After that fiasco we went back home, and soon afterwards, ITMI put together another Motown Revue for about twenty dates. I was as happy as could be—both professionally and in my personal life too.

My wife and I had been separated for a while. Before we hit the big time, we weren't making enough to support a family. The other wives kept dancing and helping out. One day Inez had told me she was going to get a job at the post office. She also said that she wanted a divorce. I didn't know it had gotten that bad. I couldn't believe it. I tried to reason with her, but she held firm. She told me that she had a guy that she wanted to marry.

After that, Mary Wilson and I started growing closer. We had a lot in common. Her hard-working mother was a domestic like mine who wanted her daughter to go college, but like me, Mary wanted to sing. She was as passionate about her career as I was. And as close to Diana and Florence as I was to Levi, Obie and Lawrence. They were like sisters. Mary was one of the sweetest, nicest young ladies I had ever met. I nicknamed her Sweet Pea because she always had a smile on her face. She would do as much she could to help everybody. Not to mention that she was as cute as pie.

Our careers started blooming at the same time. While The Four Tops were climbing the charts, The Supremes had four number one back to back hits, including 'Stop In the Name of Love.' With Motown's bounty, Mary bought a wonderful house on Buena Vista Street in Russell Woods, a beautifully landscaped area in Detroit with elegant two-and-three story brick houses. Diana and Florence lived down the street in houses that were picked out and purchased by Motown too, with everything arranged for them. Each house was distinctly different and reflected their individual personalities and lifestyle. Mary's house was always filled with people and was warm and comfortable. Knowing that I was on the road to a divorce, she asked me to move in with her, and we decided to get engaged. We started decorating it together, buying furniture and having some custom pieces built. We put in a bar and pool table. On weekends, we'd invite the whole Motown crowd over. Mary would cook a bunch of food and I tended bar for Smokey, Marvin, Martha and the Vandellas, The Marvelettes, everybody. It was like a house of blue lights, that's what we called it. We partied and partied.

I guess I was having too much fun, because one night, when Mary had cooked some delicious food for the Tops and Smokey Robinson, we heard a knock on the door. I answered it and there stood my eight-year-old daughter, Kai, who I loved dearly.

"Kai, what are you doing here?" I asked, stunned.

"My mama dropped me off and told me to ask for you," she said, as I looked outside seeing her mother drive away. Kai came in and Levi started talking to her as I got myself together.

"Why don't you go in there and help Mary in the kitchen," I finally said.

"Okay," she agreed looking around as she headed back. "You all sure are having fun here."

Kai stayed with us for a couple of days and during that time I started thinking about my children. I had a little baby boy by then too, Nazim, born in 1966. I reflected that when Inez and I had decided to get a divorce I wasn't making enough money for her. And now things were looking up. I had just had two hit records. I guess she heard from the other wives that I was getting my life together. Spending time with my daughter, I realized that my whole family needed me. So I went to Mary, the sweetest person I had ever met, to let her know what I decided.

"Mary, as much as I love you, I'm not going to be able to marry you," I said broken-hearted. "If my wife will take me in, I have to go home. I've got two kids and I just started making some money."

"Aah, Duke, don't do this to me," she said, holding back a flood of tears.

"I love you and I always will," I reassured her. "This is for me and my family. I need to take care of them."

"If it's money you want, I've got fifty thousand dollars you can have," she said with her selfless heart of gold.

"Mary, it's not about money, believe me," I told her, reminding her how much family meant to me. I realized that I'd lost sight of that, especially when music was involved. As my career grew my family had continued to expand. The Tops were like brothers to me and the other Motown artists were like family too. But my wife and children were the most important people in my life. They were my responsibility and I had no other choice but to go home.

"Maybe you're right," she finally agreed. "We're both in love with our careers. It probably wouldn't last so long."

That's where I thought she was wrong. In my heart, I thought it would probably last forever, but I couldn't stay that. I left and it broke Mary's heart. But she took it like a champ and we've always remained close. I stood by her through a bad marriage and subsequent divorce and the death of her son Pedro. Until her untimely death, we remained good friends. And she always referred to me as "the love of her life."

Inez and I got back together and tried to recapture the magic of old times. I did my best to make the hard times up to her. I gave her all my money, paid the bills, and made sure I took care of the kids properly. By then we'd been blessed with one more child, Abdul, born in 1970. I drove the boys back and forth to school each day and bought Kai a little pedal car that she pedaled to a Catholic School in the neighborhood. My sons loved the new scooters I bought them and us spending time together as a family. I did everything I could to make sure they knew "daddy was back," and promised that I would never leave them. If something changed, it wouldn't be because of me. By then the group was selling records and I'd earned some nice royalties. I bought my wife a nice little ranch style house on Seven Mile and Pennington, but for some reason she didn't really care about it. I tried to make her happy but I guess it was hard with me still traveling and not being a full-time husband or dad.

Around that time I invested in a wine bar in Detroit with basketball star Joe Strawder, who played for the Detroit Pistons. I had to spend time at my new venture to help run it. There were times when I came back to town after being on the road, I'd have to get a room in a hotel near the bar. I'd send my road manager to my house to give Inez a check or to ask her to look in my drawer for some cash. She always would, there were no complaints. I thought things were good with us but at Christmas time she disappeared. The kids and I spent the holidays without her. She didn't return until well into the New Year, and when she did she told me that she wanted a divorce.

That's when I moved out for good. I explained to my kids it wasn't their fault and that it wasn't my choice this time. It had been quite a rollercoaster ride for Inez and me. By then I had experienced some real highs in my show business career, but the price was losing my wife and kids, and I was emotionally at my lowest point. I was confused about love and relationships, questioned my past actions and decisions. I didn't think I was ready to get involved with anyone for a very long time. I guess my better angels must have taken over for me, because on the horizon was a lady who would save my life, teach me how to be a better husband and father, and show me what true love was all about. Life doesn't hand you such gifts until you're ready, and I still had a lot of growing to do first.

❧ 6 ❧

On The Road

Times were tumultuous in the 60s, especially for Black Americans. Without equal rights, equal pay, access to fair housing or protection under the law, and living in segregated conditions in the South similar to apartheid, it's a good thing that we had our music. The Motown Revue was a real sensation back in the mid-60s. When the group toured the country on the Motown bus, stopping at different cities and putting on a show with all the stars, it was the biggest thing anyone had ever seen. Audiences could see a combination of Mary Wells, Stevie Wonder, The Supremes, Marvin Gaye, The Contours, The Marvelettes, Martha and the Vandellas, Smokey Robinson and the Miracles, Gladys Knight and the Pips, The Temptations, and The Four Tops, in one night. Everywhere we went folks were dancing in the aisles. But when we hit the South, the audience was segregated with whites on the first floor and Blacks either upstairs in the balcony, or on the other side of the theater with a police guarding a rope down the middle, or crammed together in the back of the theater.

We performed at a few engagements like this until Esther Gordy complained to the promoters. She made the point that everybody liked our music, both Blacks and whites, and she objected to us performing in conditions where our fans were separated by race. Plus Black people liked to dance and they couldn't enjoy the show the way they had us crammed together in the back. Esther threatened to cancel the rest of the dates "until y'all fix this shit." And she wasn't coming back. The managers of the auditoriums and theaters tried to reason with her, they even threatened her contractually, but she stood her ground. Then she came to the artists and explained what was going on. This was during the height of Martin Luther King's influence. He had recently delivered his wonderful "I Have A Dream" speech and led the March on Washington for peace and equality. We were all okay with losing money in an effort to put an end to this kind of racial discrimination. It was difficult disappointing our audiences, but we hoped that both white and Blacks who wanted to see us perform in the South would put pressure on the theater owners and booking agents. Esther promised that she'd take care of us losing income when we went home and would book us more gigs to compensate. So mid-tour, the Revue was cut short and we headed back to Detroit knowing we had to start hustling again.

With the success of our first number one record, 'I Can't Help Myself,' released in April 1965, we started realizing that our feast or famine days might be over. We weren't going to starve. This was brought home when we signed with the ABC Booking Agency to pick up some more dates. They started out by booking us at colleges in the New Jersey area, and then suddenly there was a demand for the Tops to perform on college campuses all over the country, mostly white universities, like Purdue, Indiana, Notre Dame, Vanderbilt, and Tennessee. We were bowled over by how popular we were. When we shared this with Berry he said that he wasn't surprised. It had always been part of his game plan. He started out by marketing us to Black audiences, knowing that the Tops had the potential to appeal to white pop music audiences as well. The college crowd proved it. Soon, Berry predicted that we would become more popular with white audiences than Black ones. This was startling to us. Of course, we wanted to sell records to everyone, but we didn't count on appealing more to whites than to our own people, our core listeners, our families, our roots. After considering Berry's visionary outlook, which was to create crossover groups like The Supremes, we became aware of how important the Tops had become to Motown. We were creating a musical bridge between Black and white cultures.

And just as this crossover phenomenon had begun to set in, Esther Gordy received a call from a promoter in the South, one who had previously booked the Motown Revue. He wanted to talk about a spring booking. Before Esther agreed she asked him about the seating policy in his theaters. His response was, "Well, we kind of worked that out and your people can sit anywhere they want."

Esther was so happy to watch us return to the same venues, now integrated, and see Blacks and whites dancing together all over the place. It was a beautiful sight especially knowing that Motown had made a contribution in our struggle for racial equality. As artists, we were proud that we had played a small part in helping bring about social change. But the more I think about it, the more I realize we made a big contribution to the

Civil Rights Movement. At the same time Martin Luther King was marching down the streets of Birmingham, our music, Black music, Motown's music, was coming out of white people's basements and kitchens and bedrooms, where it had never been played openly before. People could feel and be touched by our same emotions. Whites started looking at Blacks in a new light. It didn't actually open the doors that voting and legislation did, but it did make white America a little more aware of who we were. They could better see right and wrong, that prejudice did exist, and that people were more alike than different. Whites became more open and accepting of Blacks during that period. Stereotypes and attitudes were changing. On TV they saw the clean-cut, well-spoken artists that Berry groomed. The image that the Tops brought to Motown was suave and sophisticated like Nat King Cole, Sam Cooke and Johnny Mathis, who were our role models. We regularly appeared on white TV shows like *Mike Douglas*, *Hullabaloo* and *Shindig*, the hit variety programs of the day. Eventually we were invited to perform at the Copacabana Club in New York, which only booked the classiest acts. We started appearing there the same time The Supremes did. If you appeared at the Copacabana, the top tier of the entertainment business, you'd made it, no matter what color you were. It had to be The Great Orchestrator upstairs putting all these elements together, putting things in place, making all of these amazing things happen.

Once The Four Tops crossed over the racial divide and became mainstream artists, it unleashed a floodgate of success. Things accelerated so quickly, with fame rolling in like a giant tidal wave sweeping over us from all corners of the world. *Billboard* honored us by naming it "1965's Record of the Year." We appeared on *The Ed Sullivan Show*, finally making it onto America's top variety TV program, which boosted our recognition both nationally and internationally. In the U.K., 'I Can't Help Myself' went to number two. To keep the momentum going, Berry released 'It's the Same Old Song' and 'Something About You' in the same year. When our first album, *The Four Tops*, came out in January 1965, it didn't make much of a splash. But word soon got out when our second LP, *Four Tops Second Album*, was released. Rumor had it that blew both The Rolling Stones and Bob Dylan away. Fascinated artists and fans from all over the globe made a Mecca to Hitsville USA to see where the magic happened.

Our English fans were crazy about the Tops, like Beatlemania in reverse. They referred to us as the "Gentlemen of Rock and Roll," and we were more than happy to oblige, giving us even more incentive to keep up our dapper, super-sharp image. We always liked to dress in a classic way, in outfits that could be worn on the street, not like show business costumes. But we liked to add a little flair. If we wore a tux onstage it had to have something extra, a little stripe down the leg, or an epaulet on the jacket. We always picked beautiful colors to perform in. One of our favorites was a wonderful silk jacket, each of us in a different color, white, blue, red, and gold, with contrasting pants. We wore open-collared shirts and the collar matched the pants, a two-toned color combination. It didn't look gaudy, just very sharp. Our shoes would match the pants, either black or white.

The Four Tops' sophisticated style went up a notch when we started going to England and became exposed to Savile Row and the fabrics and design in London. We started getting handmade shoes that matched the material of our suits and pants. With a powder-blue silk outfit, we'd wear powder-blue silk shoes. We started wearing shorter, trimmer English-cut jackets. We were all young and thin, and the new hip style, the pinched waist, wider lapels and flared legs, looked great on us. It really made us stand out in America where most people still dressed in ready-to-wear styles from the store. We were using the same tailors that The Beatles did, and the material and design was immaculate.

It was The Beatles' manager, Brian Epstein, who turned us onto the coolest tailors in the U.K. He was also the promoter who brought us over to the U.K. for the first time. Brian promised he'd make us as big in Britain as his Beatles were in America. We loved hearing this, but we weren't sure that we had the magnitude of music to reach that stratosphere. We had just released our biggest hit of all, and we were blown away ourselves, but we knew we needed a back-up, an even bigger tune to keep up the momentum. Frankly, we couldn't imagine a better song than 'I Can't Help Myself.' We were in for a big awakening.

When we recorded 'Reach Out I'll Be There,' another HDH song, we thought it was probably a good song for our next LP, not a single. We always thought we had good ears and could tell when we had a hit, but we sure didn't hear that one coming. We liked the harmony but it took us a while to connect

With Beatles manager Brian Epstein at the Saville Theatre on our 1967 trip to London.
PICTORIAL PRESS LTD/ALAMY

with the feeling and get into it. We just thought of it as a good experiment with Levi kind of singing and talking at the same time, like the first form of rap but with more music. Levi didn't use his natural singing voice; it was like he was doing a version of what Bob Dylan was doing, but Four Tops style. We really didn't think about it twice after we recorded it.

So when Barry called us in the office, he took us by surprise when he said, "I hope your bank accounts are in good shape. I know you've just come off a big hit with 'I Can't Help Myself' and I don't want y'all getting into tax problems."

We nodded with no idea where he was going. And he just kept going, eyes glowing. "I'm getting ready to put out a song that's going to turn the world around."

"Shit, when and where are we going to record this bad song?" I asked him.

"It's already recorded," he replied, matter-of-factly.

Levi interrupted: "What are you talking about, Berry? We ain't pre-recorded nothing close to 'I Can't Help Myself.'"

Berry smiled. "Duke, Levi, fellas, listen." Then he sang the first verse.

Now if you feel that you can't go on
Because all of your hope is gone
And your life is filled with much confusion
Until happiness is just an illusion
And your world around is crumblin' down
Darling, reach out (come on girl, reach on out for me)
Reach out (reach out for me)

Levi jumped in, laughing. "Berry, you say that's going to be bigger than 'I Can't Help Myself'? You done lost your touch, baby."

Berry joined him, laughing too. "I'm telling you, it's going to be a big hit."

I echoed Levi. "Come on, man, we've got momentum. All of our records are soaring up the charts. You put that out, it'll be number 20 with an anchor."

He had to laugh himself. But we could see he was serious and we almost started arguing with him, not believing it was a good song to follow up with. We ended up leaving his office, pissed.

About a month later, we began to hear HDH mixing it in the studio, and it was sounding better. It still didn't sound like it was going to be a big hit, surely not as big as 'I Can't Help Myself.'

Then about two weeks later, I heard it on the radio. A friend and I were in my car and the song just hit me out of the blue. I put on the brakes so fast they squealed.

"Oh, my Lord!" I said. I'd just left Motown but I headed straight back. I ran upstairs to Berry's office and his secretary informed me that he was in a meeting.

"Well, shit," I said and pushed the door open, interrupting Berry in the middle of business. "Mr. B., don't call and tell us what you're going to do no more, man. Just do it. We've got a smash!"

He laughed, "I told you," he said. "It just shot up the charts."

I told him that I didn't know what HDH added, or what I didn't hear before, but once I heard 'Reach Out I'll Be There' on the radio I knew it was a hit. It just knocked me over. For about two or three months after that, every time I heard it, in a bar or the grocery store or wherever, I'd just stop and salute the song. It just lifted the spirits. It was a mixture of pop, a Jewish chant, like an anthem or something, an enlightening song with a good message, telling friends, lovers, neighbors, whoever to *reach out and I'll be there*. Eventually, it became the number one song across the world. It was a bigger hit than 'I Can't Help Myself.' I didn't even think it would sell six copies. Neither did Levi, Obie, or Lawrence. But the other Tops were just as enchanted when they heard it on the radio. So it just goes to show, you can't always know where life will lead you. Once again we learned that there's a bigger plan at work.

The Tops had always aimed high, wanting to entertain in the top venues in the country, not imagining that one day we'd be in demand in Europe too. When Brian Epstein foretold that he'd make us as popular as the boys from Liverpool, who were an international phenomenon, we gladly put ourselves in his hands. Brian was a young man, just a little older than we were, a nice Jewish guy who was easy to talk to, free-spirited but also a savvy businessman, an expert in marketing. His first step was bringing us over to the U.K. for a promotional tour with various bookings and lots of television appearances. On the last day of the tour, we performed at a small London theater, the Saville, an eight-or-nine-hundred seater. It wasn't concert-sized, more like the size of our usual nightclub venues. Brian sold out every ticket in the house and invited key media people and artists. Backstage before we went on he reiterated his promise: "This could be great for you. You do the best show you can do, and I guarantee you will be front-page news."

The people just went crazy, and when Brian came backstage to congratulate us he was almost crying. After that he brought us back for a whole tour of the U.K. which was a complete sell-out. And in 1967 that was big, really big. To cap it off he gave us an amazing going-away party at his three-story brownstone on Chapel Street. At the party were The Beatles, The Rolling Stones, The Who, Small Faces, and every other group in the country who was on the charts or on their way up. It was a party to behold.

The first floor was for meeting and greeting, saying hello and thank you and drinking a little bit, which we all did. Paul McCartney asked about 'It's the Same Old Song,' which he was a big fan of. He told us he thought it was unique, it had a very particular sound to it, and he loved the rhythm. He said something like, "That's some bad motherfucking music." All of the artists were very nice and open, and it felt a lot like any artistic community in America where musicians gravitate to each other and shake hands and talk music. The women at the party ran up and kissed us and told us how much they loved the Tops. The guys said how much they loved the Motown sound. The thing everyone was most impressed with was how all that music could "come out of just one building." It was astonishing to them.

Moving upstairs at the party, on the second floor folks were smoking hash and weed. Everybody started gravitating up there. England had always been a little bit more open about getting high. Judging by today's standards, it may seem like it was a big drug scene. But in the 60s and 70s it was all a part of the culture, the way people partied and had mind-altering experiences. It wasn't like we were drug addicts. It was all about spreading kindness, joy, love, and happiness.

I think I was having too much fun because I never made it up to the third floor of the party. I had the driver take me home. And it was not too long after our first amazing tour of the U.K. that Brian Epstein died of an accidental overdose of sleeping pills. It was a huge, tragic loss. Later we learned that he and Berry had been in discussions about joining forces and putting together some kind of business deal that never came to pass. One of the people who worked in Brian's organization stepped up and continued promoting The Four Tops across the pond. The group returned and we did a series of concerts and remained on the front pages performing for years, just as Brian predicted. We always loved the U.K., and we always had a good time there.

* * *

Just as Brian Epstein had his finger on the pulse of British listeners and audiences, the songwriting team of Holland–Dozier Holland knew the formula for success in America, and ultimately the world. HDH were as good or better than any songwriters in the world, with ten number one songs for The Supremes alone. From the mid-60s until the 70s, Motown always had a presence on *Billboard*'s Top Ten, with often as many as seven tunes appearing simultaneously. It was just a remarkable time.

From 1964–1967, HDH produced so many classic hits that fit both the times and the artists that I referred to them not just as songwriters but as "tailors of music." They could write and produce a song that was perfect for you, and then two days later do the same thing for another artist in a totally different style. They wouldn't just write a song and after hearing it say, "Oh no, the Tops can't do this, let's give it to Martha and the Vandellas." They'd start by sitting with the artist, talking, listening, getting ideas, like measuring somebody up for suit...

Once they'd processed their ideas, they'd come up to us and say, "We got a song. We're going to play it for you to see how you like it." Sometimes, after we became great pals, we'd sit in their office while they actually created songs. Most of the time we just listened because we knew they were in the beginning of the creative process. We didn't say much. Now and again we might comment if we knew what the hell we were talking about. But they were so good and professional we very seldom commented. They were the experts. They were not guessing or trying to get it right. They knew exactly what they were looking for.

HDH recording sessions with the Tops would take about two hours. It depended on the song, what was required and how easily the Tops could pick up what HDH was trying to do. Most times it would take only two sessions, one for the group and one for the background singers, which took three or four hours. Then there would be a session with Levi doing leads, mostly two days for about two hours apiece. In less than five years, we recorded over fifteen songs with HDH. They had the biggest hand in guaranteeing our hits, defining the Tops' enduring sound and fulfilling our dreams of becoming recording artists whose appeal was not limited by race or color.

But it all began with Berry's vision. He had an ear for the market, for what people wanted to hear. He was ahead of the curve. The sound wasn't pure R&B, or pure pop; it was a mixture. When he started Motown, he told his songwriters "I want y'all to write songs that move people, that touch people and make their feet move and make their hearts beat faster. Songs that say things that people can feel and understand. Don't bring me just one type of song for just one type of group. We're making music for *everyone*." Back then that was a revolutionary concept, as unlikely as that may seem now.

This forward-thinking vision was that of a young man just starting out in the business. Although Berry had written hit songs with Billy Davis for Jackie Wilson, he had bigger goals. He was driven by the passion of youth. In youth you envision more, you dream more. Berry was able to capture that youthful energy and put it into words and music.

Berry's laser-like focus to musically cross over the racial divide was why the marriage between Motown and the Tops was so perfect. Even before Berry we never put ourselves in one box or the other. I think the Lady in White prophesized it when I was a child: "You're going to be singing for people *everywhere*". I had no idea what she meant, or that it would be a significant achievement. I probably took "everywhere" to mean generally "all over." In actuality, for The Four Tops it meant worldwide, globally and in regionally segregated America. We reached every household and radio station without restriction. That kind of reach, pre-internet, was pretty significant.

Once Berry saw how ravenous our British fans were, acting as crazy as The Beatles' fans over here, he did everything possible to keep our product flowing across the Atlantic. He seized a perfect opportunity after we'd returned to Detroit from a long tour. We headed straight back into the studio with HDH to record a soon-to-be-released album. Obviously, the songs weren't that exciting to us and we weren't singing that well. Often there were people from Berry's office or A&R people dropping by our sessions checking us out. Someone must have reported to Berry, "The Four Tops don't sound so good. They're sounding tired."

He told them, "I know them boys. They can make a hit out of anything. Guess I'm going to have to go down and wake them up."

So Berry came into the studio and sized us up. "Hey, Tops, y'all don't sound like y'all are excited. You don't have the usual vibrant sound you usually have."

That got our attention. We popped out of our lackadaisical attitude fast.

"Y'all need to sing a little more inspirational. I'm going to give you some inspiration. And I know you know how much we all like to bet."

This really perked me up; I loved a good wager as much as he did. "What kind of bet?" I asked.

"There's a great song that's beginning to gain steam by a group called The Left Banke and it's already Top Ten on America's charts. I'm going to bet you that you can't record that same song and make it a bigger hit."

That kind of challenge jolted us wide-awake.

"What is the song, and how much is the bet?" Lawrence's eyes were gleaming.

Berry threw out a great figure, baiting us, knowing a hit was in the making. I was shocked at the amount he was willing to bet. "Are you kidding, you want to bet that much on a song?" I said.

We were all looking at each other astonished and Levi blurted, "Look, I don't care what the song is, we'll take that bet."

Berry smiled seeing we were all in. "'Walk Away Renee,'" he said, awaiting our surprised reaction.

I looked at the other guys. I'd heard the song in passing, but never paid much attention to it; nothing about it seemed special.

Berry glanced over at HDH and asked them if they could work up a good arrangement. Lamont answered nonchalantly, "Yeah, that ain't nothing, it's just a good pop song."

They went off with the rhythm section and cut a track for the song and they played it for us the next day. We then went to Berry with one last question. We told him that we wanted to take his bet, but we wanted to be sure that he was going to promote the song; in essence, help us win.

His answer made perfect sense. He was smiling in that heartfelt way that's still touching to me. "I don't mind losing because I love to see your group do well." It felt like we truly were a family. Then he added, snapping back to being the shrewd businessman, "And frankly, it's good for the company. I swear I'll promote it the same way I do for all your great singles. If it's a good song, if it looks like a hit, I'll put it out there. I'll forget all about the bet." With his assurance we promised that we were going to sing the hell out of it.

The next day we recorded 'Walk Away Renee,' with HDH producing. Sure enough Berry released the song right away and sure enough, that motherfucker shot up the charts just like *BOOM*. It reached number three on the U.K. charts, and made it into the Top Twenty in the U.S., with Berry eventually having us record it in Italian and releasing it Italy where we had a huge fan base. Our version was the second most successful cover of 'Walk Away Renee' ever.

The next time we saw Berry, he said, "Well, what I'm going to do is just add the money you won to your next royalty check. Twenty five per cent of the bet goes to each one of you." Music to our ears. And once again he added money to cover the taxes.

The success of 'Walk Away Renee' was bittersweet for us, for it came on the heels of HDH's departure. In 1967 they left Motown in a legal dispute with Berry to start their own label, Invictus. The year before, they'd written and produced a string of hits for us, 'Standing in the Shadows of Love,' 'Bernadette,' 'Seven Rooms of Gloom,' and 'You Keep Running Away,' all of them charting in the Top Twenty. We were really upset when they split. HDH had given us our biggest hits; we had a winning partnership with the combination of their writing and producing and our vocals. Brian Holland could put a rhythm together that was magnetic. Eddie's lyrics touched everybody; nobody was as good as Eddie Holland for writing lyrics. Lamont Dozier would add all that stuff in the middle, those extra strains and voices that floated throughout it all with beauty, feeling, and soul. After they left, they were sorely missed by everyone. We never felt we recaptured the magic with other writers. Not just us, all the artists they worked with during their Motown run felt the same. And while HDH still produced great music, for some reason after they left Motown they couldn't buy a hit.

We were to be reunited again, ten years later, but our days with HDH at Motown were something special, like capturing lightning in a bottle.

* * *

In the 60s and 70s, there was no shortage of great songwriters in the music business. Even with Berry's great instincts there was one he let get away: a young white preacher's kid from Oklahoma, Jimmy Webb, who desperately wanted to sign with Motown. Jimmy had a small deal with Jobete, the company's publishing arm, but Berry told him he had enough heavyweight writers on Motown's label and sent him on his way. After that rejection, Jimmy kept it moving, scoring hits with 'By the Time I Get to Phoenix' for Glen Campbell and 'Up, Up and Away' for The 5th Dimension, just as he was starting his career.

But back in early '68, Levi, who was always on the look-out for great songs to record, heard 'MacArthur Park,' a Jimmy Webb song released by Richard Harris, the star of the Broadway hit *Camelot*. It was just starting to chart. Levi played it for me hoping I'd like it as much as he did. It was a unique but challenging composition. A beautiful love song written in four movements, changing tempo and structure throughout. Like Levi, I loved it immediately. It sounded like a concerto, so lush and full, like nothing we had ever recorded before. I agreed it would give us a chance to showcase our full range and abilities. When we shared it with Lawrence and Obie, they were just as excited as we were, so we learned the song, rehearsed it, and took it to Motown's music director, Gil Askey. The first thing he asked was who we could get to arrange such an complex song to do it justice. We ultimately decided on Wade Marcus, the chief arranger at Motown at the time, a producer, composer, all round talent, who was never that well known. Marcus came up with a terrific arrangement. But by the time we had recorded it, Harris's original release had become such a sensation, and there were numerous other covers that had come out by other artists, so the decision was made to put ours on our album, not to release it as a single. Still, we loved our version of 'MacArthur Park' so much that we opened our show with it when we performed live, and our audiences were wild over it. Eventually by popular demand, our version of 'MacArthur Park,' was released as a single three years later.

We loved performing 'MacArthur Park' live; we didn't need studio embellishments or recording tricks either. Levi could sing the shit out of it and when our harmonies kicked in, the whole house would just go crazy. Especially if we performed it with a symphony orchestra. Even without one, we always have nine horns; it's in our contract. Nobody could sing it like Levi. His interpretation was flawless. We pretty much stopped singing it after Levi passed. Nowadays we sometimes include it in the show and there are other new Tops, who sing Levi's part, but it never has that same effect on me. Levi's delivery was iconic.

'MacArthur Park' was one of those classic songs that our audience waits to hear. And every time we perform it, I'll be singing with tears in my eyes. I try to pinpoint why it touches me so. The lyrics are so haunting and beautiful: "*MacArthur's Park is melting in the dark… someone left the cake out in the rain… I don't think that I can take it, 'cause it took so long to bake it, and I'll never have that recipe again…*" There's always something that you once did and you left behind. You don't realize until later that it's so precious. It's a love song. Everybody has something like that. Everyone has had a cake somewhere. It also applies to whatever you know that you left, and we've all left something out there. Over the years I've had such wonderful love, but I think maybe that something from my past was Mary. I left her and I never can go back, but that's life. Now I know that there was an even greater love waiting for me. Like the lyric goes, "*there will be another song for me, for I will sing it, there will be another dream for me, someone will bring it…*"

That someone was sitting right before me in the recording studio one night, looking just as cool, calm, and collected. She was still out of my reach, I had to wait a little bit longer. I had some more living to do to be ready for her, but soon my passions would "*flow like rivers through the sky,*" as Jimmy Webb so beautifully put it.

❧ 7 ❧

The Road To Raging Fire

One of the greatest songs of the twentieth century, 'What's Going On', wasn't a Four Tops recording, but we were there at its inception. One of the Tops, Obie Benson, co-wrote it with Marvin Gaye and Al Cleveland. 'What's Going On,' an R&B classic that crossed over into pop, rock, and whatever category wanted to claim it, is honored by *Rolling Stone* magazine as one of the greatest songs of all time. It is truly a reflection of the times. As artists we were witness to the horrors that were happening all around us. Our musical expression gave voice to what everyone was feeling. In the late 60s and early 70s, people were constantly shaking their heads, shocked and stunned by each new occurrence. Our cities were burning, the war in Vietnam was escalating, young people were protesting in universities across America. The Civil Rights Movement which started in the late 50s used picketing, boycotts, and demonstrations in the fight for equal rights. Now their tactics were used by Women's Lib and the Peace Movement. All over the country, folks were rising up, protesting, marching, and sitting in. Discord, discontent, violence, and destruction were right outside our door on a daily basis and on the TV screen every night. Our boys—it seemed like a disproportionate number were Black— were shipped home in body bags or returned to their families maimed and psychologically damaged. Funerals and memorials were an everyday occurrence. On top of that, some of our most beloved leaders, true visionaries, were assassinated, locked up or run out of the country. Folks lived in a climate of shock, denial, pain, and fear.

In 1970, with all the crazy shit happening around us, the Tops had just wrapped an all-night recording session, where we were cocooned and insulated from what was going on in the streets. We joined Smokey Robinson for a few holes of golf and stopped off at Marvin Gaye's house to unwind. We were all very close, living only a few blocks from each other. Our work, which we were passionate about, flowed seamlessly into our personal lives; it was all one and the same.

Even though what was happening in the real world sometimes seemed far away from our lives as Motown stars, we had family and friends who were directly affected by the war. Racism was a fact of life for all of us. That night we were kicking back, drinking beer, talking about our golf game and Obie was going on and on about the state of the world. He'd just seen some police brutality go down on 12th Street. He was fussing about it and asking what the hell was going on. Marvin, as usual, was sitting at his piano picking at the keys, fooling around. His brother Frankie had just returned home from Vietnam and told him about what was going on in Southeast Asia. He told Marvin what most Black G.I.'s were saying at the time. It made no sense to be fighting over there, losing our lives to spread freedom and democracy, and at home where we were supposed to be free, we were denied our rights and losing our lives too. Marvin was feeling what Frankie and Obie were echoing. And

Obie could be very adamant about things, very passionate in his convictions, and he kept going on and on.

All the while, Marvin was picking out a melody on the keyboard. Obie kept encouraging him, saying, "yeah, yeah that sounds good…" Obie started laying the words on top of the music, "*what's going on…*" Marvin told him to keep on saying it. So for about ten to fifteen minutes, Obie kept repeating the same thing over and over, talking about how he felt, and Marvin kept putting music to it. They kept at it for at least an hour before I had someplace to go. I left and the next day Obie told me about this song that they'd just finished writing, "What's Going On." He said it was going to be a *bad mama jama*. That was the last I heard of it until they recorded it.

Then one day I heard a playback of it while they were mixing it in the studio. I remember telling Marvin and Obie how soulful it sounded. All the people in the studio were saying the same thing, it was a baaad song. Meanwhile, Obie kept working with Marvin on other songs for his album. When it was completed, the next decision to be made was which song would be released as a single. Berry didn't approve of Marvin's pick, 'What's Going On.' Marvin and Berry had a big fight over it. Berry was adamant that he didn't want any kind of political protest songs representing Motown at the time. He said that Motown songs were about love, joy, and happiness. Music that people could dance to. Marvin argued that 'What's Going On' was special. It's what people wanted to hear. Berry insisted that it wasn't the kind of message that Motown should be putting out. He was in the business of selling songs, not making social commentary. This went back and forth with them almost coming to blows. Finally, after a couple of weeks, they worked out some kind of deal. It didn't hurt that at the time Marvin was married to Berry's sister, Anna Gordy. She must have been instrumental in helping Berry realize that he should give Marvin his creative freedom. To Berry's credit, he was able to constructively hear other opinions, so he backed down. And the rest is history. It turned out to be a great, great hit. Much bigger than just a song. It was like an anthem, a plea for help, a meditation. And it still is.

'What's Going On' tapped into the universal question people all over the country were asking. Everyone needed answers. It was an intergenerational, racially inclusive message that reached everyone. You didn't just have to live in an urban area to be affected by what it was saying. You could be in rural America, the heartland of the country, and still be shaken by the enormous upheavals and changes rocking the planet. But somehow for me what was going on sometimes seemed very far away. In my mind, the Detroit riot of 1967 wasn't as earth-shattering as people made it out to be. I was aware it was happening. At the time we were in the studio recording. Our focus was beyond what was happening just a few blocks away. I knew that people were looting and burning and rebelling against bad conditions. It actually felt more like a social upheaval than a riot. In the end, I saw there were some improvements as a result of it. Some of the old buildings on 12th and 14th Streets, from Clairmount to West Grand Boulevard, were torn down and rebuilt, which was good. But philosophically, my head just wasn't there at the time. Probably it should have been, but it wasn't. I was lucky. I'd sit on my porch drinking wine or champagne, and just shake my head. This was at the peak of our careers. I was busy thinking about what we had to do in the studio. Where our next tour was going and all of that.

The riot that had the most impact on me occurred when I was a kid, in 1943. Racial tensions in Detroit during World War II reached a peak with the KKK having a stronghold among newly arrived white migrants from the South. They were indignant about Blacks competing with them for the same jobs. Housing conditions in the Black sections of town were overcrowded. Nearly a quarter of a million Blacks lived crammed together in sixty square blocks on Detroit's East side in an area known as Paradise Valley. At the time, some neighborhoods were still racially mixed with working class whites. We had Italian neighbors, who worked in the factories living across the street from us.

Fighting between whites and Blacks broke out at the bridge near Belle Isle Park one hot summer night. It rapidly spread throughout the city. I lived on Cameron and Owens on the East side. Sitting on my porch I watched unspeakable acts of violence and brutality play out right before my eyes. Groups of armed whites from outlying neighborhoods travelled to the Black side of town to attack residents. Black residents jumped on them and fought back. I saw a white guy get his throat slit with a razor. White mobs overturned cars owned by Blacks and set them on fire. They beat Black men as white policemen just looked on. It was just horrible. At the corner people were fighting inside the Clairmount streetcar. Rumors and stories circulated among both Blacks and whites about atrocities perpetrated against them and kept the violence going. The rioting seemed like it lasted a week. For an eight-year-old kid, it was like forever. It actually took two days before federal troops were called in. Then it went to another level. I saw soldiers shoot a Black guy out of a tree. A white doctor was beaten to death while making a house call in a Black neighborhood.

It finally took six thousand soldiers to put an end to it. I might have been a kid but I was not too young to know what was going on. I was almost crying it was so bad. All this horrible stuff occurred around the time I couldn't force the words out of my mouth, singing praise to the Lord in my grandfather's church. It was when the Lady in White came to me with assurance, saying everything would be alright. Maybe to let me know that singing was my ticket out of there.

My hometown going up in flames in 1967 might not have affected me outwardly, especially with all the good things happening in my career, but my alcohol consumption increased at the time. Perhaps it was a sign I preferred not to think about the hard stuff. Instead, I partied it up, living in an altered state. That was when I was part-owner of the wine bar on Livernois Avenue. I drank so much I used to eat a half of stick of butter before I left the house to line my stomach so I wouldn't get sick. I would drink from ten o'clock in the morning until two o'clock the next morning. It all came with running a popular bar whose customers wanted to hang with an entertainer and a sports star, my co-owner Joe Strawder. Everybody in town started hanging out there, entertainers, night lifers, professional folks; it was a great mixture. My years watching Daddy Braggs manage and run the Paradise Club in Idlewild paid off. My life revolved around entertaining, hanging out and recording. I was happy, I thought that was what life was all about. I wasn't looking to make any changes or take on any serious commitments. I had been married, and it didn't work out. It had brought me much grief. My life was arranged just the way I wanted. I had it all under control, or so I thought. Until I met Piper.

To put it bluntly, after I divorced I vowed, "I would never ever get in that shit again." I had been burned by my ex-wife. I knew that I wasn't perfect either, but I wasn't looking for another wife. In fact, I was actively turning the other way. But there she was, sitting in the studio watching us record, expressionless, nonchalant. Most girls would be making eyes, trying to get you to look at them, but she was just sitting there. I didn't know at the time, but Piper Gibson was the most popular girl in her class at Cass Technical High School, a prestigious, academically challenging high school in downtown Detroit. She had been voted the Prettiest Girl in a racially mixed class of over five hundred students. Not only was Piper beautiful with golden, caramel colored skin, dark hair and doe-shaped eyes, she was accomplished, ambitious and smart, having just completed a year at Spelman College. She had recently returned to Detroit and enrolled in the University of Michigan. Piper had always had her pick of boyfriends. Her attitude was blasé and aloof. Unimpressed.

After my first glimpse, I asked Denise Gordy, Berry's niece, who was hanging out with her that night, to make introductions. In all my travels, to meet someone who was as good-looking and classy as Piper in my hometown was intriguing. Frankly, I'd never met anyone like this young lady, and right away I could tell she was the whole package. I wasted no time in inviting her to return to the studio for another session as my special guest.

Piper came back a couple of nights in a row. Finally we went out, just the two of us, to a nice supper club, Mozambique. After a couple of drinks and something to eat, I looked at her and said, "You know what, Piper, I'm going to marry you."

She laughed, not taking me the least bit seriously. "You know what, Duke, you're crazy."

"Well, that's what's going to happen," I told her, in all seriousness. I knew I was not letting her get away. Back in that day, badass, sexy Blaxploitation sisters were up on the big screen, super-heroes like Pam Grier. Piper was in definitely in that category. She took no prisoners. From the very start, she captured me.

I seriously started courting her. I took it as a wonderful challenge to win Piper's heart. The more I saw her, the more I talked to her, the crazier about her I got. On the road I'd call her after the show. We'd talk long distance for two or three hours every night. It felt like young, first-time love. Maybe I'd never really been in love before, because I could tell this was different from my earlier relationships. The "Duke" I was years before would never have gotten to first base with Piper. She set the bar high with strong values about family, education, life, and love. As we got to know more about each other I could tell that she was getting serious about me too. However, she revealed that our relationship probably wasn't going to work out.

"My mama doesn't want to meet you. I can't bring you home."

I'd never encountered this situation before. Everyone I met was crazy about knowing one of The Four Tops. "Well, how long do you think this is going to go on?" I asked.

"I don't know. My mama doesn't want to hear anything about me dating someone in your business. She doesn't think much of show-business people."

Piper's mother, Sarah Gibson, was a well-regarded school principal in the Detroit public school system with a doctorate in Education. She had raised her two daughters, Piper and her younger sister Kyle, almost singlehandedly after her divorce from Piper's father. Providing for her girls, making sure that they were well educated and culturally exposed, was her top priority. Sarah, Piper, and Kyle lived in a beautiful townhouse in a new development in downtown Detroit along with an integrated group of doctors, educators, lawyers, politicians and the like. Diana Ross had recently purchased a penthouse apartment in one of the condominium high-rises. The only other show-business type I knew in the area was Eddie Holland's mistress, Jamie, who lived a few doors down from Piper, in a lavishly decorated townhouse. The other neighbors politely regarded her as a "kept woman." Certainly, Sarah didn't want Piper mentioned in the same breath.

So Piper and I courted for a year or so in secret before her mother even knew. Still, our relationship kept growing and Piper kept working on her mother to get her ready for an introduction. Finally, one day in 1972, she said, "Okay, my mother is ready to meet you." She was nervous. They were very tight;, she respected her mom and didn't want to go against her. "Duke, you've got to be on your best behavior."

"I'm happy to meet her," I said. "Don't worry, here's what I'm going to do. I'm going to come in your house cooking. I would like to prepare a dinner for her, a meal like my father does."

Piper liked the idea and told her mother she had invited me over for dinner.

When I arrived at their house, Sarah and I exchanged pleasantries, then I told her that I'd like to make an Indian meal for her. She replied with a sassy laugh, "So get your ass cooking then." She could be funny. I made chicken curry with curry green beans, and cut a watermelon in half and diced it all up. I made a whole meal and all the trimmings while she watched and listened to me tell her about my life, letting her know what being a performer was really like. How we recorded, where and why we toured, how the money worked, all the inside, serious business stuff. I could see she was impressed, like she was thinking to herself, "…*well he ain't dumb, that's a relief.*" I could also tell that she'd heard a lot of negative stories about entertainers, and she expected me to be her worst nightmare. But by the time we had finished eating Sarah and I were the best of buddies.

One other thing I did was show Sarah how serious I was about her daughter's future. It sealed the deal. Right before the night was over, I put my money where my mouth was. "By the way, Piper, I got this extra money here," handing her over four thousand dollars in cash. "I want you to open a safety deposit box for you and me down the line," I said.

As Sarah watched me hand Piper a wad of bills, I explained

to her, "You know your daughter is going to be well taken care of, don't worry about it."

"You got all this to spare?" she asked me.

"I got a good day job," I told her jokingly. I was honest and up front about my commitment to my ex-wife and children. I explained it all to her, summing it up by saying, "A lot of my money goes to different places. I've got a family and I do right by them. I have enough money for what I need to do. If your daughter wants to come along with me, I'll always take care of her and give her the very best."

That night I won my future-mother-in-law over. From then on that I started coming over to their house almost every day. Sarah and I were great friends for over forty years until the day she passed away. But Sarah wasn't the only one whose objections I had to overcome. There were lots of people who predicted this was going to be a two-week affair. It hurt me that my Four Top brothers didn't give us a month. They saw our relationship as a match between a show-business guy and a cute little scholarly girl who had nothing in common. One of the guys actually had the nerve to say to me, "You're going to marry that skinny bitch?"

I shot back, "First of all, she ain't skinny and she ain't no bitch. You're talking about the woman I'm going to marry. I would never say that about your wife."

He quickly backed down. "Yeah, well I didn't mean it like that."

I was pissed, but I knew where they were coming from. They were still friends with my first wife, Inez. Their wives had been tight since their Ziggy Johnson days. All they could see was that Piper was young and beautiful. I reassured them that there was

Marrying the love of my life, Piper, in 1974.

much more to her than that. Yes, she was good looking, but she had what it took to be my girl forever. I'd finally found my *Sugar Pie Honey Bunch*.

The prediction I made on my first real date with Piper, that I was going to marry her, came true in 1974. A year later we welcomed our beautiful baby daughter, Farah, into the world. It was a good thing that I got a chance to start over to build a strong home life to sustain me. Little did I know my Motown family was soon going to come apart. The string of hits like the ones we enjoyed in the mid-60s and early 70s were no longer guarantees. Our next releases were hit and miss at best.

❧ 8 ❧

The Road West

There were some acts at Motown that received special treatment, given more attention than others. Of course The Supremes were Berry's most prized group. When Diana Ross broke out as a solo artist, The Supremes were downgraded to second tier level. The Temptations, Smokey Robinson and the Miracles, Stevie Wonder, and The Four Tops were pretty much the acts that Motown put out front. That all changed when The Jackson 5 arrived in '69. Their youthful act was a game changer. It was around that time that the company decided to make a major shift, gradually moving its headquarters to Los Angeles. Berry had conquered the music industry, now he set his sights on getting into the television and film business. Some say the Detroit riots in '67 also gave him the impetus to escape to the sunny vistas of Southern California. The new challenges and the chance to reinvent Motown with a bright, upbeat identity appealed to him.

Not everyone was motivated by those new horizons. The vow that the Tops had made to stick together forever was put to the test when Berry tried to get Levi to break away from the group like Diana Ross had done. His strategy was to take the lead singer, move him into being a solo act and keep the original group going at the same time. He was shocked when Levi, who was the key to this strategy, wouldn't go for it. He made a big play for him initially.

From L.A. Berry called Levi on the phone and pitched to him: "I've got a part in a movie for you. Would you and your wife like to come out here to talk about it?"

Levi agreed, hung up, and called me; we always discussed things since we were kids. It all sounded good to me, I told him he should go see what Berry was talking about. Berry flew Levi and Clineice out to California. They were picked up at the airport and whisked to Berry's house. Berry enthusiastically described the movie he had in mind, *Lady Sings the Blues.*

"I got a wonderful part for you. You'll be playing the romantic lead opposite Diana Ross who's going to be portraying Billie Holiday. The part is perfect for you, it's written for you." He was referring to the role of Billie's husband, Louis McKay, eventually played by Billy Dee Williams.

Berry kept talking up the movie, trying to appeal to Levi with how much money he was going to pay him. It was a great deal. Berry went on and on and Levi got really excited. Finally Levi asked him, "What about the Tops, what about my boys? Is there a part in it for them?"

"Naw, man, this is just for you," Berry told him. "I don't have a part for nobody else."

Without a moment's hesitation Levi replied, "We're going home then."

"What do you mean?" Berry asked, genuinely surprised.

"If you don't have a part for my guys then you don't have a part for me. It's the four of us or nothing,"

Levi walked away. He and Clineice went straight to the

airport. He wouldn't even let Berry's people call for a car to take them.

When Levi got back to Detroit, we discussed what was going through his mind when he turned down that amazing offer. Levi said he could see breaking up the group as the next step. Levi didn't care about the money. He didn't care about none of that. He was already famous with the Tops. To him that was famous enough. He didn't have an oversized ego. All throughout our career, Levi had several other offers from record companies and people who wanted him to go solo. He'd always tell them, "No, thanks, this is our group. We grew up together. We made a commitment. We love what we do just like it is."

Levi's instincts were right about the movie being a move to break us up. Inevitably, Motown came to Levi with the idea that they wanted to rename the group Levi Stubbs and the Tops. Again, it was something he'd never go for. He had that kind of loyalty. Our group came to realize it was one of the things that folks loved about us. We were a group who stayed together. Unity and brotherhood were qualities that people admired. Our fans often marveled, "You guys always stuck together no matter what." It made us proud that we had values that people respected and could relate to.

The decision about us leaving Detroit and moving our families to Los Angeles when Motown left was a difficult one. We loved our hometown, were proud of our roots and the city's rich history, despite the hard times it was going through. The previous five years hadn't been our happiest or our most productive period. We'd scored a hit with 'It's All in the Game,' produced by Frank Wilson, and a beautiful, haunting tune co-written by Smokey Robinson, 'Still Water (Love).' It was a big record and helped sell our album, but our future was filled with uncertainty. We were pretty certain we weren't going to uproot ourselves to follow Motown to the West Coast, especially with the way things were going.

By 1971, the year after we recorded 'Still Water (Love),' we still were not happy with what was going on with Motown. We weren't really in the studio as often as we wished. We had recorded a couple of albums, but times were changing. We could feel our momentum slipping. We'd been scuffling since Holland, Dozier and Holland left. We needed to get some hits. When we finished our last album for Motown in 1972 *Nature Planned It*, we noticed that the promotion we were accustomed to wasn't there, especially with the single releases. Since this was also near the end of our contract, we needed to renegotiate. We thought it was a good time to see what was going on. Going to Berry's office, we discovered that he had turned over the presidency of the company to Ewart Abner, Stevie's manager. Berry was now chairman of the board. He wasn't really on the scene running the company day to day. Most of the time he was in Southern California focusing on expanding the company with other show business ventures. The official announcement about Motown relocating hadn't been made public yet. The Detroit offices, the staff, and operations were still in Detroit being phased out.

We went to meet with Ewart Abner and brought up a few

things we wanted in our new deal, specifying the right kind of advance, a certain amount of money per album, designated promotion dollars, and all that. By then we had learned a little bit about business. As we were talking about promotion, Abner stopped us. "Hold it right there. We've got a lot of artists out here now. You kinda have to wait your turn. You know how it is. It's like we promote this one and that one…"

"We thought we were one of your key artists," I cut in, knowing how things worked at Motown. "Key artists are supposed to get promotion whenever their record comes out."

"Well, you're not one of our key artists anymore."

We were blown away. "What do you mean by that?" I shot back.

"There's another artist ahead of y'all at this moment that we're working on. You have to wait your turn."

While we were processing that, he decided to drop a bigger bomb.

"You guys have had a great run. This is as far as you can go with Motown, that's it," he said out of the blue. "We don't really need you guys anymore."

We looked at each other in shock. I mean really *shock* shock.

"It's over for the Tops. Y'all are free to do what you wanna do, go anywhere."

We were speechless. None of us knew what to say. I was so mad and hurt. Not just about what he said, but the way he said it. So matter of fact. Cold, like he was throwing out the trash. I was so pissed "the street" in me almost came out. I wanted to hit that motherfucker in his eye, but I held back because that's not the way Motown had treated us. It had been good up to that point, no gangster stuff. None of us confronted him even though we were devastated. We walked out of his office with our heads up, but we went somewhere and almost cried. We were heartbroken.

"What the fuck are we gonna do?" we wailed. Amongst ourselves in private we always questioned whether we were as good as we thought we were, or if being under Motown's umbrella was the thing that helped us succeed and survive. After some quick reflection, thinking back to our previous successes, it didn't take us long to rebound.

"Well, shit, maybe Motown ain't the only thing going. We know we're good. Fuck 'em. Let's go out and get a deal."

That same day, one of Motown's promotion men, Larry Maxwell, heard about what happened and came to us, saying, "Man, that's awful. Berry should hear about this."

"That's alright, man," I told him. "Nobody's talking to nobody around here anymore."

"If they let us go, case closed," Levi said. "We're going to find something else."

"I'm going to California as part of a promotion," Maxwell told us. "While I'm out there I bet I could get y'all a record deal."

"Go ahead, man, see what you can do," I said. What would it hurt?

Two days later, Maxwell called. "Duke, y'all gotta hear this shit I found for you. A couple badass songs by writers on ABC/Dunhill's label, Dennis Lambert and Brian Potter."

Maxwell returned to Detroit with one of the writers and a tape of the songs. He played 'Ain't No Woman (Like the One I've Got)' and 'Keeper of the Castle' on a little cassette tape recorder.

"*Shit,*" we looked at each other blown away, "*these are some bad songs!*" They were raw, but we were so experienced with recording by then that we could hear what a full production might sound like. We agreed to meet with the President of ABC/Dunhill, Jay Lasker, to discuss some kind of deal. This required that we go to the West Coast to meet him face to face. The songs were worth it. So off we went to California. Ironic, because Motown had asked us to move out there, and now that's where we were headed.

We sat down with Jay Lasker in L.A. He started talking about a four-album deal. Obviously, he was excited about signing The Four Tops. He was making a real commitment. He told us that it would be nice if we moved out to the West Coast to record, so we had to explain that we'd already been through this with Motown. We weren't going to leave Detroit. Agreeably, Lasker said he'd send for us to record. He would put us up in the Beverly Hilton, which we suggested. He agreed to pay for the hotel and all expenses while we recorded. It sounded good. I asked him how much we were going to get for each album. Instead of him coming up with a figure he asked me how much we wanted. It was hard for us to say. We hadn't come up with a figure beforehand. I just threw out one hundred thousand dollars an album. He asked his lawyer to quickly do some figures. He countered with fifty thousand. I told him that he had to do better than that. We eventually agreed upon sixty-two thousand, five hundred dollars per album, but we had to own some of the publishing rights. We knew this was what Berry was contractually giving his artists now. Lasker agreed to half of the albums being written by his writers, the other half of the albums would be ours. This would enable us to create our own publishing company with those royalties coming to us. To sweeten the deal he made us an offer to set up our own recording label in a few years, which was exciting both creatively and financially. We'd be able to control our own product, sign new artists and expand businesswise. We accepted, eagerly looking forward to the new growth and possibilities many top recording artists were contractually being given that time. Lasker said he could make it happen if we got ourselves a good attorney to draw up the correct papers. We agreed to this, shook hands, made a deal that day. Lasker was pleased but told us that the contract wouldn't be ready to sign until later on, but he'd have it to us before we delivered the first album. He'd pay us half up front so that we could get going. We felt great about the whole deal and were rarin' to go, especially since we knew we had two hit songs in our pocket.

We started in recording our first album with ABC/Dunhill immediately. As soon as we finished recording both songs, we sat down with their quality control people. We decided that 'Keeper of the Castle' should be the first single out the box. It wasn't the stronger of the two, but it had the same kind of driving rhythm and beat that people associated with the Tops. Then we'd drop the second single, 'Ain't No Woman (Like the One I've Got)', a

In our best black sequinned blazers...

...And red crystal ones, early 90s.

With my wife, Piper, late 90s.

Piper and Whitney Houston.

In the studio for one of the final times with the four of us, mid-90s.

Performing with new Top Ronnie McNeir, Glasgow, 2002.

The 2008 iteration of The Four Tops, at the Gibson Amphitheater, California.

A proud day, collecting our Lifetime Achievement Grammy Award, 2009.
MICHAEL BUCKNER/GETTY

With Smokey Robinson at the Motown Museum, Detroit, 2013.
JEFF KAROUB/AP/SHUTTERSTOCK

With the West End cast of *Motown the Musical*, Shaftesbury Theatre, London, 2016.
DAVID M. BENETT/GETTY

Piper and me with Berry Gordy, backstage at *Motown the Musical* in Detroit, 2017.

Celebrating my granddaughter Najma at her high school graduation.

With the current Four Tops line up, 2019. (L–R) Lawrence Payton Jr., Alex Morris, Ronnie McNeir, and me.

My daughter Farah and her husband, Ralph, with their three children, Justin, Riley, and Carly.

Doing what I love most, 2014.
ANDREW BENGE/GETTY

post-Motown comeback with a one-two punch.

Sure enough, according to plan, 'Keeper of the Castle' opened the door fast and wide. It hit the top ten on *Billboard*'s national charts. The album with the same name started flying off the shelves. After that, we put out 'Ain't No Woman (Like the One I've Got).' That motherfucker became a hit the minute it came out. It soared all the way to the number four spot, the highest we had been in years. It eventually became another Gold Record for us.

It felt good to be back on top again, disproving all the naysayers who had predicted our careers were over. Especially Ewart Abner who we hoped was taking note about how much money our new album was raking in. I finally was able to have some peace about how my mother felt about my music. I was never really comfortable with her thinking I was singing the "devil's music." I knew it pained her. So I invited my whole family to come watch us perform at the Roostertail Supper Club in Detroit right after 'Ain't No Woman (Like the One I've Got)' was released. They were all excited, sitting in the front row and eating dinner. My mother and I had just finished our meal, I turned to her and told her I had to go backstage to change into my uniform for the show. The next time I saw her face I was onstage singing. I could see her out in front staring up at me, only a few feet away. She was totally expressionless for the first two or three numbers, but by the time we reached our fourth number she was smiling the nicest, biggest smile. I could tell she had finally accepted what I was doing. She could feel in her heart that my music was spreading joy and happiness. It wasn't church music, but she was really loving it. It was another day to add to the happiest ones in my life.

I missed my other family, my Motown family, so while we were working on our ABC/Dunhill recordings in L.A., we would go over to visit their new headquarters as they were settling in. We were upfront with Jay about our ties over there, and clear about our allegiance to our new record company. I told him, "We belong to ABC/Dunhill now and we're gonna do everything we can possibly do to be the greatest artists you ever had. But we will always be a part of Motown's family."

Jay was cool about it. "As long as you keep promoting ABC/Dunhill and doing everything you can to sell records over here, that's all I ask. I know where your heart is."

One day Berry heard we were visiting Motown and he called us. "Fellas, why in the fuck didn't you call me when Ewart Abner said he was letting you go?"

"Didn't you know ahead of time what Ewart was going to do?" I asked him. "Don't you all talk?"

"No, listen to what I'm telling you, man," Berry explained. "I never would have let y'all go. How could I let you leave? I never imagined he'd do that." He sounded as upset as we had been.

"Listen, Berry, at that time we were so devastated," I explained. "We were in a state of shock. I was so upset I didn't want to talk to nobody. All I wanted to do was get out of there."

"You should have called me, man," he said. "All you had to do was call me."

"I'm so sorry we didn't do that, Berry. You know we still love Motown. That's why we're over here now. We love everybody here," I said, now apologizing to him about what happened.

"Tell you what, anytime you want to come back, just call me," he assured us. "The door is open, front door, back door. You just have to say the word."

Berry made good on that promise later down the road. After talking to him it really felt like he didn't have anything to do with Ewart's decision. We knew he had been busy moving the company to L.A. and making his movies. So we chalked it up to being one of those unforeseen things that happen and focused on making it work at ABC/Dunhill.

Our first album, *Keeper of the Castle*, was a big seller, and shortly after its release we finalised our deal. We had hired a California attorney and had gone through all the legal steps. It took about six months and fifty thousand dollars to get it all set up on paper.

After *Keeper of the Castle*, we enjoyed moderate success with the next two, *Main Street People*, in 1973, and *Meeting of the Minds*, in 1974. As we were finishing our fourth album, *Night Lights Harmony* in 1975, it was time to meet with the company to sign a new contract and see if we could go forward with our new record deal. We went directly from a recording session to present our label proposal to Jay. In the meeting we were surprised to see a Black guy, Otis Smith, the newly appointed head of Black promotions, taking an active role.

We handed Jay the papers. He only looked at them a second, then passed them to Otis saying, "I don't really believe you

Celebrating twenty-one years together in 1974.
MIRRORPIX

fellas still want me to go through with this."

"Yeah, man, you said all we had to do was get the papers correct. We're on our last album. In our new deal you said you could make this happen."

"Well, fellas, I got to tell you, I really can't do it. I can't give you the deal," Jay said to us.

I asked him why. Otis Smith stepped forward and said, "I'll tell you why, 'cause y'all ain't ready for this shit. You got that Detroit swagger and all, but you're not ready to be the kind of businessmen it takes to take care of this album."

"What you say, nigga?" I walked over to him, grabbed him

by his collar and dragged him through the president's office. "Motherfucker, I'll throw you out this window." He looked outside to the sidewalk below. We were up on the fourth floor. The fellas were right behind me. They didn't say nothing, it was like, "*If Duke's going crazy, let him go crazy!*"

"You'll cause us a lifetime of grief telling Jay that," I said, shoving him up against the ledge.

Of course, I came to my right mind and I didn't throw him out. Afterwards, when we got back in Lasker's office, he wrapped things up by telling us, "You sure ain't gonna get a label now."

"Well, fuck you too, Jay," I said, heading to the door. "We'll finish this album. We don't need your help to finish it, goodbye."

We went back in the studio and finished *Night Lights Harmony* ourselves. Lawrence and I mixed it. We helped master it. They put it out. But they really didn't put it out, they gave it no promotion and it died. Afterwards, they released several other Four Tops albums with material that we had recorded under contract to them. By then we were gone.

Once again we were looking for a new label. After sustaining insults and doubts regarding our ability to handle business matters, we were undeterred. Soon after, we met our longtime manager Rod Strasner. Ron began his career as an architect. Eventually, he started managing Martha Reeves. When he reached out to us about management, I told him I wasn't interested, all we needed was a record deal. Ron said he thought he could get us a deal with Casablanca, a big-name record company at that time run by Neil Bogart. Neil passed away right after Ron talked to him about us. One of the guys still there, Dave Koppelman, was still interested. He had his songwriters present us with some songs, among them 'When She Was My Girl.' It takes good songs to make a record deal, and we took to that one right away. So with Ron's efforts, we made a deal with Casablanca, landed ourselves a new manager, and got a nice little advance.

With David Wolfert producing, we made a great album, *Tonight!* David captured Levi's lead vocals beautifully. He was great at blending all our voices together. Even with the past commercial sounds of Motown, our harmonic vocal sound hadn't come through as much. As a group this was our unique strength. We all loved the way *Tonight!* sounded. We had a lot of fun recording those songs, some in L.A. and some in New York City. Again, we felt very good about our new label. Casablanca released 'When She Was My Girl' as a single. Right away it took off, becoming a number one R&B hit. It almost made it into the U.S. pop Top Ten, peaking at number eleven; in the U.K. it went to number three. Both the single and the album sold very well. It brought us back into the fold immediately. By then the ups and downs of the business were to be expected. We entered each new deal and business relationship with a healthy dose of faith and skepticism. But meeting Ron Strasner turned out to be a blessing.

We recorded another Casablanca LP with David Wolfert producing, *One More Mountain*. From that album came the song 'I Believe in You and Me,' a lovely ballad. It was big on the East coast, in New York and Philadelphia, but unfortunately it didn't catch on in the South or the Midwest. Although the radio stations played it, it didn't reach the charts. Even so, 'I Believe in You and Me' is one of the most beautiful songs we have ever recorded. A lot of people use it as a wedding song, and we still use it onstage, along with a couple of other great songs from those two Casablanca albums.

In 1983, in the midst of our time at Casablanca, a Motown reunion was in the works. Berry wanted to get all his people together for a televised 25th Anniversary special, *Motown 25: Yesterday, Today, Forever*. It included a segment produced by an impressive top level Motown executive, Suzanne de Passe, who also produced TV and Film, and Gil Askey, the arranger we had brought to Motown, with the Tops performing onstage with The Temptations. As we sang, we were trying to one up each other, trading songs in a little battle of the bands. In rehearsals it felt good. When it was televised it came off really beautifully, the highlight of the show—until Michael Jackson came onstage. We'd loved it when he performed earlier in the show with The Jackson 5, but when Michael came out by himself, it was mind-blowing. He just turned the whole damn thing out, performing 'Billie Jean,' doing the moonwalk. It stole the whole show, forget everybody else. Diana Ross was good. Smokey was good. But when Michael took the stage, everybody was in amazement. He was going crazy. The look, the dance, the feeling, it was just everything. We were all ecstatic.

Over the five days we rehearsed *Motown 25* at the Santa Monica Civic Center, we only had two dressing rooms. The women had one big dressing room and the men had the other one. For that whole week, we hung out with Marvin Gaye, the Jacksons, the Temps, The Miracles, and other artists. We all had so much fun in that dressing room. They should have had a camera in there for extra footage. The shit-talking, the fun and the jokes were non-stop. At this time, all us Motown acts had gone our separate ways; we hadn't been close for some time. We were all out there busily doing our own thing. The show felt like a big family coming together for a reunion or Thanksgiving. All the guys were playful kind of guys, making bets, pulling pranks, playing poker. We won a little money, things happened that I just can't talk about. It was crazy fun.

Michael mostly kept to himself, but every now and then he'd pop in the dressing room and say, "…you guys are crazy." Once, in a quiet moment, he approached Levi and told him that he listened to our songs when he awoke in the mornings and simply loved his voice. But generally, he was so quiet that you hardly even noticed him. Most of us hung around the majority of the day, watching each other rehearse, commenting, going back to the dressing room, messing with each other, and just being together. It was refreshing.

When we saw Berry (who didn't really hang around rehearsals), everybody had a chance to say hello and reconnect. Berry approached the Tops personally, saying, "Hey fellas, y'all sounding great and looking great. Y'all ready to come back?"

"Yep, we sure are!" We were more than ready.

"Well, after this get in touch with me. In fact, I want to record you and the Temps on a song. I'll have someone write something for you. I'd like to do another couple albums, guys.'"

Soon after that, we did go back to Motown one more time. After our first album, *Magic*, was released in 1985, Berry felt something was missing. He wanted us to start working on another album. We suggested collaborating with Holland–Dozier–Holland again, asking if we could use them to write and produce. Lamont had split from the HDH partnership and Berry was still in the midst of a legal battle with them. All of their issues hadn't been resolved. But Berry didn't object, saying it was up to us to get them back together if they agreed.

I called Eddie. He'd written some songs for us on when we were at ABC/Dunhill. I'd always stayed in touch with Lamont. Every time I went to L.A. I'd go over his house for a good meal. He could cook as good as any chef. So I went over to talk and eat. They all agreed to get back together to write for the Tops. Once again, they wrote us some beautiful songs. The album was appropriately titled *Back Where I Belong*. It included a song with Aretha Franklin, 'What Have We Got to Lose,' which Berry just loved. It should have been released as a single; it was just romping and reflected that Levi and Aretha were very close friends. Together they were a perfect vocal match. The album also had several other great songs, including the title song, 'Back Where We Belong', and 'I Just Can't Walk Away,' a ballad with a nice feel. But before it came out, Eddie and Berry got into it again, another falling out. Motown eventually did put the album out, but they didn't really put it out. No real promotion or anything. We were so mad and disappointed.

We'd finally gotten our dream team together against such difficult odds and our efforts still hadn't panned out. It showed us again, there is no magic formula. So much of success is out of your hands.

Even after all that we went back to Motown one more time. I went to Berry's house and asked him about the songs that we recorded years ago for our Broadway album. Maybe there were a couple of great songs that we might be able to release right away, I suggested.

"I don't think so, Duke," he admitted. "But I'm going to search the catalog to see if there is something we missed that we might be able to put out there. I still believe in you guys. I know you can make some hits." But nothing really happened.

We were out of ideas to resuscitate our recording career. Our manager, Ron Strasner, wasn't discouraged. He went to Clive Davis, the head of Arista records who was an acknowledged music industry wizard, best known for making the career of Whitney Houston, Dionne Warwick, among others, even having a hand in Aretha Franklin's success. We played him some of the tracks that we'd made at Motown, particularly 'Indestructible.' Clive loved the song and made a deal with Motown to acquire the tracks. He released it under Arista's label. He did an amazing PR job for our album with the same title. Clive sent his production people along with us to southern Spain to promote the album, where he rented an amazing villa for us to perform what he predicted would be a global hit. I'll never forget the villa because he told us that if we walked one mile across a bridge we'd be in Northern Africa. None of us took the time to do it. It would have been great. Later, when Sun City was built, the Tops were invited to perform in South Africa at their new arena. We thought about it. The money they offered us was great, but because of apartheid we didn't go; politically we just couldn't do it. We'd played all over the world—Japan, Hong Kong, Macau, Belgium, the Netherlands, Germany, Italy, France, Denmark, Sweden, Brazil—but, sadly, we never made it to Africa.

Despite Clive's best efforts promoting 'Indestructible,' something about that song just didn't hit. He even put two of his best producers on it; one of them had produced for Whitney Houston. Clive also made the first video we'd ever done for a release. It helped the song make a little noise, but it never became the hit that we wanted, or that Clive predicted it would be. It had such an upbeat, positive message that it was used in a campaign to promote the 1988 Olympics. Even that international exposure didn't sell the song. Our relationship with Arista was a good one. However, after being on so many different labels—Chess, Columbia, Riverside, Motown, ABC/Dunhill, Casablanca, and finally, Arista—it was the last record deal we ever had.

The disappointment of 'Indestructible' led us to an unexpected fork in the road. We were so sure that 'Indestructiblc' was going to be a hit, especially with Clive Davis and Arista behind us. We started wondering if it was the end of the road for us. There we were with no map to guide us, no longer at the top of our game, no longer young or idealistic. This was where the road split off in other directions. We knew that the Tops were indestructible.

There was nothing that could separate us as a group, but each of us had different things to take care of. Before we took off down our own paths, we were given two amazing signs that things weren't over for us yet. We still had lots of life to live, just not in the ways we had expected.

🪶 9 🪶

The Road Back Home

There we were thinking we were at the end of our careers, maybe even feeling sorry for ourselves. Then we got a wake-up call: life wasn't just about having record deals and earning gold records. Singing had always been our passion, but it became apparent there was so much more we had to do. It was a time of new beginnings, fresh starts not endings. Lockerbie was our first reminder.

It was around Christmas 1988 and we were in London doing *Top of the Pops*, which was the UK's top TV variety show. We were scheduled to tape two segments, one before another group that was booked on the show, then another the next day. We wanted to switch our performance schedules so we could get back home during the holidays. We hoped there was a flight going to the States with enough seats for all of us. Our travel agent checked, found out it was possible, and told us to make preparations. We were so sure that we were going to be on that flight that we called our families to let them know we'd be on the plane due in from London the next day. Then we tried to talk the producer out of keeping us that extra day. We begged him to switch our schedules so we could do both segments the same day. We told him we needed to see our loved ones, go shopping, and do our Santa Claus thing. When he wouldn't let us go, we were heartbroken. We even offered to do quick costume changes, whatever it took to make it happen so we could get on that plane. He said he wished he could accommodate us, but he just couldn't. He wouldn't budge. We had to wait one more day. We were so mad at him.

Later that night the phone started ringing with calls about a plane crash over Lockerbie, Scotland. That was the exact flight we would have been on, the biggest plane crash in recent history. A bomb on board had detonated, killing all two hundred and forty-three passengers, sixteen crew members and eleven people on the ground. We all looked at each other and said, "It looks like the Lord's got more for us to do." We felt so lucky, we almost kissed that producer the next day when we went to work. He knew that we had been really pissed at him. "Be happy because you all would have been gone," he said, relieved also.

If we'd gotten our way that day, the Tops would have been gone in 1988. Our epithet would have been ...*down in Lockerbie.* This was our sign that it was nowhere near our time to go. When we got off the plane two days later in Detroit, all kinds of newspaper people and reporters were waiting for us. But we didn't feel like talking. I said, "Look, I'm devastated about what happened. It was a tragedy, but I'm very happy that I'm home. I can't wait to start sharing Christmas with my family." And as the New Year rolled in, I was grateful to be alive. I realized that *I might be down but I'm not out.*

This sentiment was reinforced when we were notified that The Four Tops had been voted into the Rock and Roll Hall of

Fame. An act can't be put on the ballot until twenty-five years after their first record, and we were put on the ballot twenty-five years after the release of our first hit record in 1964. We were told that the vote, among our peers, had been unanimous, which felt wonderful. We were among a very elite group of our fellow artists honored that year, among them singers Hank Ballard, Louis Armstrong, Simon & Garfunkel, The Four Seasons, Bobby Darin, and The Platters.

The induction ceremony took place in the ballroom of the Waldorf Astoria in New York, and to our great surprise the artist who introduced us was Stevie Wonder. What a heartfelt tribute he gave. Any doubts we had about our place in history or our musical contribution were chased away by the love and respect given to us that night. Accepting onstage, we even sang a little a cappella number to let everyone know we still had it. Even we were impressed reading the program notes which said, "…between 1964 and 1988, the Four Tops made '*Billboard*'s Hot 100' chart forty five times, and its R&B chart fifty two times. Twenty four of their singles made the 'Top 40' and seven of those entered the 'Top 10.' The only thing than can outlast the Four Tops' line-up is their incredible body of work."

That recognition from our fellow artists helped us reconnect with what we knew in our hearts. Something we'd lost sight of when the record execs told us we had no more value. We were *loved and appreciated*. We had created a body of work which no one could take away from us. Our loyal fans all over the world would pay to hear us perform. We went back on the road

All together for our Rock and Roll Hall of Fame induction, 1990.
ROBIN PLATZER/GETTY

touring, giving concerts, booking engagements, and singing in front of live audiences. Something we loved doing and had done from the very beginning. We'd started out singing in a basement house party in Detroit and built our career from there, long before ever setting foot in a sound studio. Having come full circle, it was time for us to spread our wings and explore different possibilities. I decided to try my hand, once again, in the restaurant business.

Just before Lockerbie, The Four Tops had been honored by Governor Blanchard of Michigan, who declared June 18th

1987 as "Four Tops Day." We were invited to Lansing, the state capitol, to meet dignitaries, receive a nice tribute, and take a tour of the Governor's mansion. I brought my mother along with me for the day. She was especially thrilled when she got to sit at the Governor's desk in his big chair. I could see her shaking her head, thinking she'd never seen the day. On the radio we'd heard the proclamation that it was Four Tops Day. Our music was being played non-stop. At the end of that wonderful day, when I took my mother back home, she was almost crying.

"Mama, you were the first one to tell me to sing. Remember you made me sing when I was a little boy?"

She just sat there shaking her head, too overcome to speak.

"This is your glory too," I told her. It had been almost fifteen years since she'd first heard me sing with the Tops at the Roostertail. We'd come a long way since she'd given me her approval. Now at the Governor's mansion she saw how far I had come. She wasn't with me the next year when we were inducted into the Rock and Roll Hall of Fame. In fact, at that time she was close to passing. Being inducted into the Hall of Fame was probably one of the few things that could have pulled me out of the dumps with her health failing. She died not long after that. But in that moment, we could savor Four Tops Day, both of us probably reflecting back to when Central State University had given me a college scholarship and I'd blown it off to sing. We just sat together, feeling what we didn't have to put into words, knowing how much we'd both been blessed.

The next day something told me to reach out to Governor Blanchard for a helping hand. I'd been waiting to hear from the Comerica Bank about a loan application Piper and I had made to build a house in the Palmer Woods section of Detroit. We'd been looking at houses until we realized that we would be better off designing and building our dream home, rather than renovating one. Piper had designed a gorgeous house and was working with an architect drawing up plans. Now we were just waiting to hear from the bank. I'd been introduced to the head of the Bankers Association of Michigan at Four Tops Day. I asked the Governor if he could put me in touch with someone to try to move the process along. Within twenty-four hours, the bank called to tell me our loan had been approved. We were ecstatic, grateful for the blessings that came as a result of my music. We were also grateful that we had been shown love from the state and city which enabled us to build our dream house in Detroit. We'd always felt a loyalty to our hometown. We wanted to demonstrate that by investing our money in the city and raising our family there.

That sense of giving back to the city also fueled my desire to make an exciting investment in a floating restaurant on the Detroit River. The *SS Lansdowne* was a historic barge that had once ferried vehicles back and forth between Detroit and Windsor, Canada. It had been converted into a two-hundred-and-ninety-four-foot restaurant with two dining rooms, a banquet hall, and a sky top lounge, which we envisioned turning into a casino. Bringing gambling to the city was a direction Detroit was headed in an effort to bring income; after many people fled, the tax base had eroded, and the car industry was dying.

My cousin Darnell Kaigler, a respected dentist in the area, was interested in restoring historic boats. He presented me with the possibility of being his partner in this restaurant and banquet business. Even though the restaurant had been shuttered for a while, I could envision the Lansdowne as an exciting spot for nightlife on the waterfront. Piper didn't agree with me. It took lots of convincing to talk her into it. Ultimately, she gave in. Probably because she could tell I was really excited and needed a project to throw myself into, since I was no longer spending long nights in the recording studio. Plus, it would only be open on weekends, which seemed manageable.

Darnell and I signed a lease putting up the initial investment with Mayor Coleman Young helping us to get an additional grant from the city. I put everything I had into making it work, including getting the best Cajun chef I could find to come to Detroit from New Orleans to create a delicious authentic menu. We made sure each one of our dining rooms and the jazz lounge downstairs was decorated beautifully. A huge aquarium filled with exotic fish ran the entire length of the room downstairs. Our wait staff were well-trained by our excellent general manager. We had him vetted and felt confident he could handle our ambitious venture.

The food was so good we had many faithful customers from all walks of life. One of our regular customers would come to the back door of the kitchen every Saturday night with her own iron kettle for the chef to fill up with Lansdowne's special gumbo. Even Aretha Franklin, who was a great cook herself, loved our cooking. I felt so proud to help create a top-shelf, unique dining experience in downtown Detroit during its hard times. But after a year of operations and support in the community, our floating venture was tanking fast. Despite all of our preparations and the considerable cash infusion my cousin and I were making out of pocket each week, we badly needed financial help. Luckily, Darnell found a local businessman with available funds and business ties that we didn't really question. He gave us over a million dollars to help resuscitate the business. It wasn't until after the Lansdowne's closing that he was arrested for dealing narcotics and we discovered the truth of his questionable business dealings. Our association with him came under scrutiny. Luckily, I had been careful not to associate with him directly or give him a requested partnership in the business. I'd kept my distance.

I could not believe that what started as an innocent business venture became so detrimental. It put my family, my standing in the community, and my career at risk. Fortunately, the hard lesson I had learned years before, when I had gambled away the earnings belonging to the + 4 musicians, was seared into my consciousness… *never take what doesn't belong to you*. I was able to substantiate that I had not misappropriated funds or used any of our investor's money for my personal use, and that I had no business ties to his other dealings. I could account for every single penny which had been borrowed solely by the business for the business. I had not taken one dollar for myself. Thank God, I came out unscathed by telling the truth, not hiding anything, and providing an honest accounting of my records. I humbly came out of the Lansdowne experience only too happy to refocus all my energy back into the group. And also, knowing more than anything, I needed to listen to my wife.

* * *

Piper had been after me to stop my drinking for quite a while. She was always like an angel on my shoulder. But I didn't take her advice right away, promising that I'd stop when the time was right. Finally, one night I came home drunk and she confronted me. "You're going to have to make a choice. Either you're going to give up drinking, smoking blunt, or whatever it is that you're doing, or you're going to come home and we won't be here. You have to become a real husband and father."

God knows I didn't want to lose her. We'd had our ups and downs. That's life. But I knew I wasn't going to let anything take her away from me. She's the reason I'm alive today. If Piper hadn't come along, I would have eventually killed myself one way or another. Not intentionally, just self-destruction. Too much life, too much show business, too much being out there. Piper balanced it. She came at the exactly right time. I know God sent her.

Meanwhile, Piper and I had been looking for a church home. We'd been to about five or six different services trying to find the right one. Piper's mother, Sarah, suggested that we attend the African Methodist Episcopal (AME) church she was going to. We went with her one Sunday morning and enjoyed it immensely. Everything felt so familiar, the service, the choir, and especially the Reverend and his wife, Dr. and Mrs. Reverend Gregory Ingram. She was the assistant pastor, and they both had a wonderful way of communicating the message. Piper and I remarked to each other how much we liked it. After a few weeks, she joined. I hesitated, saying I needed to think about it for a while. I just wasn't ready yet.

Around that time, I had a show in Las Vegas. I was getting ready to party in my room one night with a group of friends, a bottle of Courvoisier, some cocaine and some weed. Out of the blue, a voice in my head spoke to me, *"I'm tired of this shit man. This is not me."* I proceeded to kick everyone out, knowing, *"I just can't do this anymore. If I don't stop now, I'm never going to."*

Thank God I never went past cocaine. Never did, and never would. None of The Four Tops did. Growing up around the North End in Detroit, there were a lot of heroin addicts. I was always fearful of that fate. I'd heard that once you shoot up you might as well keep going. Just one shot, that's all it takes. I did start liking cocaine, however. Everything was so vivid. It makes you want to just keep going. You wanna drink more, smoke more, make love more. But you begin to enjoy it too much. I know that I did. That night in Vegas I reached the point where it was now or never. I had to back off from it.

When I got home, I told Piper that I'd made up my mind. "I'm not drinking, I'm not smoking. This is it, case closed." But I knew I needed strength. I got down on my knees and prayed, "Lord, I need your help." I prayed and prayed.

Then I heard His voice: "*I will be with you in this house for a while.*" I know it's hard for people to believe, but it happened. Like I've known all through my life, I know He's been there for me. That's how I stopped drinking. Just like that. I didn't drink another drop of alcohol for almost twenty years. After that, only a glass of wine or champagne now and then on special occasions.

A week later, I joined the church. The first order of business was attending a class for new members. When they handed me the book detailing the history of the church, I almost fell to the floor. Staring up at me was the name Virgil Landis Eckridge, my grandfather, the founding pastor of this very church. Oak Grove was a name that I had remembered hearing as a kid and I associated Oak Grove with a place, not the *name* of the church. Plus the church had moved, my memories of it were distant, but they all came flooding back. I remember my family talking about my grandfather starting his church in little tents on Wyoming and Seven Mile Road, then a mostly rural area. AME was founded in the tradition of the English Methodist churches in the 1700s. The first congregants pitched tents for their services out in the wilderness. Oak Grove was my grandfather's first church back in the 20s. After initiating the church in the tents, they moved into the first Oak Grove AME building on Cherrylawn and Pembroke Avenue, where my granddaddy was the first pastor. Now, here I was, over half a century later, finding my way back home. If that wasn't affirmation, I don't know what is.

I began to see my life as a mosaic of pieces coming together in a story that had already been written. The Lady in White foretold it outside my grandfather's church when I was just a little child, while he was inside preaching the word. It was there that the vision of my future came to her. And everything she told me has come to pass. She didn't say that I was going to be popular *in Detroit,* she said *the whole world. The whole world is going to love you.* It was astonishing to me then. Now, as the years go by, it becomes more and more astonishing.

After I joined the church, in 1994, I told the pastor I wanted to be an active member. I didn't want to just sit there on Sundays and enjoy the service. Plus, I knew that working in the church would help me with what I was fighting against. He asked if I wanted to sing in the choir. I told him that I'd love that, but I wouldn't be able to attend most of the rehearsals, and I'd feel bad just walking in and singing without doing what was required of everyone else.

The next week he called me into his office after the service and asked me if I'd heard of his Men's Ministry outreach group, "Master's Men." He said he wanted me to head up the Ministry as a facilitator, along with a younger man named Milton Weathers, the son of a preacher, who would help me. I thought he was kidding, telling him that I was no preacher. The Reverend explained that the role didn't require preaching. It was teaching men how to be better men, better family men, better husbands, better men on their jobs. Oak Grove needed something to attract more men to the church, to make it more exciting, since the congregation at that time was made up of mostly women. "I believe the men will follow you," he said. "All you have to do is just read this little booklet. Your first meeting will be this coming Tuesday." I went home, read the booklet, tried to bone up, and talked to Milton on the phone a few times. We decided that we'd talk about being good parishioners in our first meeting on Tuesday and follow up with a Prayer meeting on Wednesday.

At that very first meeting, the Reverend introduced me and had me open with prayer. I had never prayed out loud in front of people before. It's totally different than praying to yourself. I stopped two or three times, not knowing where to go next. I just said things that came into my mind and the Reverend said that I did okay for the first meeting. I was relieved, until right away he gave me another assignment. He asked me to speak at a drug and alcohol rehabilitation center called AmeriTime the next week. He wanted me to tell them my story, how I put my trust in the Lord and so forth. That was too much like preaching, I told him.

"If you put a band and three guys next to me, I'd probably be okay," I said, trying to joke my way out of it.

He kept reassuring me: all I had to do was talk about my life. I could write down what I wanted to say on paper. People would respect me for just being there. They knew who I was, they'd listen to me. "It's something about you. I think men will follow you," he said.

I followed his advice, went home, and wrote out my speech on what had happened in my life, how I'd just stopped drinking, and giving advice about what to do, and what not to do. When the day arrived, I went up to the podium shaking like a leaf. I had my paper in front of me, but it was all handwritten. Even though I had on my glasses, I couldn't see the words that well. For a minute, I froze. Then I took a breath and just told them who I was. I started talking and I must have talked for a good fifteen minutes about the things I'd done. How the Lord came into my life and helped me. I told them that it wasn't too long ago that I had totally given up drinking and drugs. I was one step away from being in the chair next to them. I told them how easy it was to get out of that chair with faith and religion. Apparently my speaking went down so well they asked me to come back and speak the next week. I had to admit to the Reverend that I wasn't as uncomfortable as I thought I'd be. He said his instincts were right, reaffirming that I had what it took to be a good teacher and leader, especially for Black men.

Working as the facilitator of Master's Men became a very important part of my life. Growing into that role, becoming a good leader, I started volunteering in the church kitchen on Sunday mornings. I cooked and served the ladies who ate breakfast there before the service. They would look at me knowing I was a Top, wearing an apron, being their waiter, and just nod their head approvingly. Serving them, being a humble man, I was brought all the way down to being a real servant of God. The Lord really gets to you one hundred per cent by serving people. I was still a singing star, but even if I was working out on the West Coast, I'd catch a red-eye to get back to church on Sunday morning. Everyone praised me for that. I loved what I was doing. I started a Walk-a-thon for the church and began the biggest fish fry in Detroit. Most of all, I enjoyed working as a facilitator for Master's Men. While I was there, we had eight ministers come out of the program. All of these men have churches of their own now, including my own son, Nazim Fakir.

Being the child of an entertainer isn't easy. For the parent, it's difficult when you're on the road, or recording. You believe that the music is everything, that your career, or your life's work, should take precedence. When you finally realize that there is nothing more important than just being there for your family, it's usually too late. Your kids are grown. They've moved away. You've missed out on forging that relationship which you both needed. My three kids Abdul, Nazim and Kai were adults by the time I started being aware of this. When they were young, I paid for their upbringing and I tried my best to guide them, to get them out of scrapes, and to help them get good educations. Each one of them had their own challenges. I was grateful that when Piper and I had our beautiful daughter, Farah, I was more aware of what being a good father meant. And that Piper was such an amazing mother.

Nazim was the son who was always getting in trouble as a young man: DUIs, kicked out of high school, dropping out of Florida A&M University (with a full scholarship, he was so smart), getting locked up for drinking. I tried everything I could to help him. I got to the point that I was pretty much through with him. But there he was sitting at Master's Men in my second week as a facilitator, listening attentively. I could see that he enjoyed it. After a few weeks, he actually joined the church. He seemed to be getting a lot out of it, but I couldn't have predicted what happened next.

"Dad," he said, "the Lord has called me to preach."

"What do you mean preach, where does he want you preach to at?" I couldn't help but laugh.

"I'm not kidding. The Lord has called to me to preach many times, but I've been running. I don't want to run anymore. I want to be a preacher and I'm going to preach for the Lord."

I realized he was serious. I told him I thought it was wonderful. He'd already made this great AME connection, but he'd have to go to college and finish his degree.

"Oh, I'm going to do all of that, don't worry," he said. "I'm serious."

So we prayed on it right then and there. And sure enough he went to the University of Detroit. He signed up and got a degree in business, while all the time working with a mortgage company. Nazim graduated with high honors. From there he went on to Garret Theology School in Chicago, where he got his Master's degree. The only thing that stopped him from finishing his doctorate was pastoring his first church in Chicago. It was in bad shape and needed to be resuscitated. He did such a great job that he was given the pastorship of a large congregation in Minneapolis. He still leads it successfully and is a prominent minister and leader in the community. One of his many important contributions has been starting a medical program to support people with diabetes, helping them to lose weight. A challenge that he himself overcame, a diabetic losing over eighty pounds.

I guess you can say it was in his blood. His great-grandfather, my maternal grandfather, Virgil Landis Eckridge was an AME minister. His grandfather, my father, Nazim Ali Fakir, was so devout that he fought to raise his kids as Muslims. Though my mother won the religious battle my father never gave up his faith in America. He attended the mosque faithfully.

It was really gratifying that at the same time I was turning my life around, embracing God to help me give up drinking, so was my son. That's when it hit me that he had always been following me since he was a little baby. I hadn't been aware of it. He'd follow me in his mind, and even into bars I went to. As a young boy, he was trying to learn from me about how to be a man. Not until I started leading the "Master's Men" did it all come together for him. And for me.

It made me think back to the day when I felt I became a man myself, by honoring, respecting, and taking care of my family. I was in my twenties, and it would be a few more years before we'd sign with Motown. Times were still hard. Me and Levi went to my dad's apartment. "Dad, I need some money," I said, knowing a lecture would be forthcoming.

"Yeah, fucker you always need some money," he said shaking his head. "You hang around at night with these gangsters. I know a lot of people that will work for peanuts, but I don't know no motherfucker who'll work for peanut shells."

He didn't think much of my ambition. He knew that I was

trying to sing, but he hadn't come to hear me yet. But he gave me the twenty dollars I needed that night.

A few weeks later, when we were singing at the 20 Grand, he was sick, but he came to see me anyway. He, too, finally approved: "You can sing good. I hope you make some money, man." I bought him a lot of drinks that night. It was the last time I saw him and he was happy. He always kept ties to his roots, but I didn't know that he was soon going back to Bangladesh, where he married a sixteen-year-old girl. I was relieved when I heard he was living well back there. A couple years after he left came the sad news of his passing away of cholera.

As I didn't get a chance to say goodbye to my father, I went down to the Indian clubhouse in Detroit where he and his friends would hang out during the week and eat dinner together on Sundays. I asked them how I could do a ceremony to honor him here, a burial rite or a memorial. At first, they didn't understand; they told me that no one did that for their family members in this country. I insisted, it's what I wanted to do. That's how much I loved him.

In chatting with Bill Kabbus, the owner of the 20 Grand, I mentioned the journey I was on to honor my father. He said he would introduce me to a Caldean priest who might be able to assist me. The priest agreed, but first, I would have to find a pure lamb and personally watch him cut the lamb's throat, spill its blood, and make sure it was cooked a special way. He took me down to the Eastern market to find a pure lamb. I paid for it and watched him cut its throat, next, it was loaded onto a truck and taken to a butcher shop to be skinned and cooked.

I accompanied it to make sure that it was taken care of the way I was instructed and that it would be delivered to the feast properly.

The next day, my whole family, my sisters and brothers, and all of my dad's old friends gathered together at the Indian Clubhouse. The priest said a prayer and told the guests that this was the first time he knew of someone in this country doing this for their father who went back home. He raised a toast, "praise this young man." Then we had a big feast. The meat was so good. After that I felt so strong, like I could do anything. I remembered a verse that I'd learned in church, "*Honor thy mother and thy father, and your days will be long upon this earth, which the Lord thy God giveth thee.*" I became such a confident young man that day. It felt like I had grown at least a foot. All that day people thanked me, saying how great a man my father was, how much he loved his children. He hated to leave but he had to go home. I understood. Somehow I knew it was my place to give him a homegoing worthy of him.

It would have been nice if I could have done something like that for Billy Eckstine. He was like our dad in show business. Billy picked up our education where my dad left off. At that moment in our lives, we were young men needing guidance. He handpicked us to do the supper club circuit with him. When we went to Motown, we returned the favor. We brought him along with us, trying to help him revive his fading career.

We had just signed with Motown and approached Berry with another deal. Since he told us that he wanted to start a jazz label, we asked, "How would you like Mr. Billy Eckstine?"

Berry's eyes lit up. "Oh man, he's a great singer. He's like Sarah Vaughan and the rest of them. I'd love to have him." So Berry signed Billy. When his album was finished, something went wrong. Billy cussed him out. He was getting to that part of his career where he was really angry about the way he was being treated. He was over at Berry's house and said exactly what was on his mind. Then just walked out. He ended the relationship just like that. Billy Eckstine was a brazen kind of guy. He didn't take shit from nobody and he was mad at show business. Frank Sinatra was coming up at the same time he was. Billy was just as talented, but as a Black singer he didn't get the same treatment. He still made a great living, but all that stuff started to wear on him. Eventually he lost his beautiful wife, his kids, the amazing home he built in Las Vegas. As good as he was onstage, he was very hurt about all kinds of stuff. He started taking a lot of dope and got addicted to drugs.

In his last days, when we were performing in Vegas, he'd come to our show and sit with us and talk. He'd tell wonderful stories, then ask "…you got $500 on you?" Things got so bad, we had to pay his bills for the last two or three months before he passed away. The whole jazz community mourned him, acknowledging that Billy was one of the greatest singers we'd ever had. Duke Ellington called him the "essence of cool."

Lionel Hampton said, "We were so proud of him because he was the first Black singer singing popular songs in our race. He was one of the greatest singers of that era. He was *our* singer."

He was so cool even Quincy Jones wanted to emulate him. "I looked up to Mr. B as an idol. I wanted to dress like him, talk like him, pattern my whole life as a musician and as a complete person in the image of dignity that he projected."

But Quincy also understood the pain Billy had to endure in the 50s, "If he'd been white, the sky would have been the limit. As it was, he didn't have his own radio or TV show, much less a movie career. He had to fight the system, so things never quite fell into place."

Because our group came along a decade or so afterwards, we were able to follow the trail he blazed for us. We reaped the rewards from battles he fought. Billy taught me one of the greatest lessons I learned in show business, if not, *the* greatest.

One night in Lake Tahoe back in 1962, the house at Harrah's was full, and he called me backstage. "Duke, look out there," he said, as we looked out over the audience. "What do you see?"

"Man, it's a full house," I answered.

"Look again. Look closer."

I stared out over a sea of people. "They look like the same faces I see everywhere, it's beautiful. Mostly white people."

"Here is what you see," he said, his eyes filled with love. "Those people out there, they've been taking care of me, my desires, my family, ever since my first record, 'Jelly Jelly.' If you get a chance to get maybe a million fans, Duke, take care of them. 'Cause if you do, they will take care of you for the rest of your life." He had a tear in his eye. "They've been taking care of me no matter what I've done all my life. Whenever you get a chance pat them on the back, love them, don't play them cheap, because they will be your life—if you're that fortunate, and I know you will be."

I never forgot that and I never will. I pass it along to the youngsters who ask me for advice about making it in this business, what it takes. I tell them, "Guts and blood. The blood is your hard work, your sweat, your tears. Your guts is going past your fear, your inner doubts and what people tell you you can't do. But more than that, it takes love. You gotta love what you're doing. You gotta love singing or performing, whatever it is that you're doing, you gotta love it. You gotta be committed to your last breath." But as much as you love the music, in order to survive, there must be something more.

I've given a great deal of thought to what happens to great artists like Billy Eckstine and Michael Jackson. Why did Michael feel like he needed to be so high? Or Prince, any of them. I think that as youngsters they come up with a gift or a talent and that talent takes over. As they move up in the world, they lose their childhood, their youth, and they become whatever the music is. Whatever that drive is that keeps them going. They never get to experience what they're really like *without* the music. They live only for the music and the times onstage and in the studio. It becomes their whole life. The other part of their feelings, just being themselves, is overtaken by the creativity and the music. Whenever they're not onstage they are looking for something to give them that same feeling, so they turn to dope or something else. They don't understand the raw feeling of being *who they really are*. Because who they are in their minds is the music. That's what their mind is telling their body. They take drugs to recreate that great feeling in their normal life, but they can't fill that space. They have to learn to live *outside* the music.

Looking at the great singers of our generation, so many of them suffered with alcohol or drug addiction: Sam Cooke, Teddy Pendergrass, Jackie Wilson, Prince, Whitney, Marvin Gaye. Each one of them is different, their lives unfolded in different ways, and it happened at different stages in each of their lives, according to their bodies, their minds, and where they were in the business. But somewhere along the way that unhealthy part of being a musician or singer, that imbalance in their lives, took over. And it was stronger than the natural part.

I came to my senses just in time. I eventually realized the greatest high I could get is from the love, not what I put in my body. The applause and the looks from the audience of respect and love and thanks. That's what makes me feel better than anything. That's the high I want to feel. And I had to learn how to feel good without the music. Getting sober allowed me to constantly reveal to myself who I really am. I am a loving family man. I love my family. I love being at home making my wife, children, and grandchildren happy. I know that for me there are two separate worlds, my music and my home life, and I've learned to enjoy them both. I got close to thinking it was all one. I separated just in time. I thank God for giving me the strength to say, "I can't do this anymore. This is not right. I don't feel right." And I think that has something to do with me still being here.

I've talked this over with Otis Williams, the last surviving member of The Temptations. Otis was always the leader of that group, he still is. We've talked about us both surviving, both still performing. How we've managed to stay alive. Two of the greatest singers in the original Temptations, Eddie Kendricks and David Ruffin, couldn't survive the business. In 1968, during Motown's biggest days, Eddie and David decided to leave the group. Obie and I tried to talk them out of it. We were all great friends. They each had their personal reasons. They also didn't like how the money was being split among the group—following orders, to be honest. In every group there are disciplinary rules that you have to accept. There is usually one member who sets up the rules. It's usually not democratic, but it has to be done. They felt they were big enough to make up their own rules.

Once the Tops and the Temps were on the Motown Revue tour together, and instead of riding with everyone else, David had himself a limo. We were buddies and sometimes I'd ride with him, partying, drinking, doing a little coke. We once caught a parking valet in Norfolk, Virginia, trying to steal clothes from the car. We beat him up right in front of the box office. David wanted to stab him (like back in the day, gang fighting on the streets in Detroit), but I stopped him before he lost it completely.

David was a good guy. He loved being around people, performing, hanging out, but as loving as he was, he had a pompous side. I called him "Lord Jim," because he carried himself like he was some kind of royalty. But he did it in a nice way, without being totally arrogant.

Eddie, on the other hand, didn't talk a lot. A nice low-key, simple guy. When he wasn't high or having fun, he was just kinda quiet. He could sing really well. He had a beautiful tenor voice. In fact, Eddie sang the tenor part for me for the recording of 'Bernadette,' when I was not feeling well.

We tried to talk Eddie and David out of leaving The Temptations, we loved them, they were like brothers. We'd climbed the mountain of success together. Obie and I tried to impress upon them that they had spent their whole lives working to get to this point: "Are you kidding? You came from a hole in the wall and now you're world famous!" We gave them all kinds of examples, like that they should be able to put up with any small annoyances to keep making such good money. We talked to them like preachers, like brothers, whatever we could think of. They still wouldn't listen. They both left the group at the same time, each recording solo albums at Motown. After a year or two, their careers were in free fall.

Often, if the world loves you as a member of a group, when you leave, you're just not as strong as a solo artist. Something is lost. You lose your way. Especially if the group keeps getting higher and higher. You're out there by yourself, left behind, all alone. David died of a cocaine overdose in 1991 when he was just 50 years old. Eddie lived just a year longer. His cause of death was listed as lung cancer, but many believe that drug abuse was also a contributing factor. I attended the funeral in his hometown of Birmingham, Alabama, which built a beautiful park memorializing him. An earlier member of the Temps, Paul Williams, one of its founders, died years before in 1973, when he took his life after being kicked out the group for drinking. All of the Temps were such sweet, talented guys. Too much living, too young.

Losing good friends, fellow singers, from that golden era in our youth reminded me that life was short. It scared me to think that if I had not stopped drinking, doing drugs, and partying, I might be the next one in the dirt beside them. The question of my mortality loomed in the back of my mind. It was something I would soon have to confront despite my best efforts to turn my life around.

❧ 10 ❧

The Lonely Road

We were on the road traveling, performing onstage and slated to open at Caesars in Las Vegas when Levi got to feeling bad. Lawrence wasn't feeling well either, so we cancelled. We had never worked at Caesars before so I was a bit let down, but the guys really weren't up to it. A three-week rest was what Lawrence's doctor ordered, so I had time on my hands to kick back with nothing scheduled. It was Piper who decided that it might be a good time to get myself checked out too. I resisted. I felt fine, I told her. It hadn't been so long ago that I'd cut out drinking and smoking. I was in great shape. But she insisted. Since I'd married Piper, she'd finished her undergraduate degree and her masters, graduated from law school, passed the bar and become a prosecutor for the City of Detroit. I should have known better than to argue with her.

My doctor gave me a thorough check-up. He examined my heart and decided that some further testing was necessary. I was blown away with what the cardiologist discovered. I had a ninety per cent blockage in two of my arteries and a seventy per cent blockage in another one. There was no question that I needed heart surgery. While I was processing this, my wife decided to find a different cardiologist. I don't know what prompted her, but she started doing research and found a Dr. Sakawa to perform my coronary surgery, which in 1995, wasn't as commonplace as it is today. The first heart stents had just started to be used in 1985 and a triple bypass was a big deal. It was a good thing that Piper was handling all this because I was paralyzed. The idea that my chest would be cracked open, my heart taken out and put on ice while my arteries were repaired, was terrifying to me. But I had no other choice. I had come this far, made some major changes in my lifestyle, and had a new lease on life. I knew that God hadn't brought me this far to turn his back on me now. My heart might not have been working at full strength, but my faith was stronger than it had ever been. I believed in my heart that I had a lot more work ahead of me. I was thinking all this on the operating table as I was saying my prayers and started counting backwards…

* * *

When I came to, my pastor, Piper, and a few other people were standing around me. I opened my eyes, barely conscious, and saw tubes running everywhere. I opened my mouth, trying to make a sound, "…*aaaaa, aaaa…*"

"Duke, what is it? What are you trying to say?" someone asked.

I managed to reply, "I'm making sure I'm still a tenor."

"Negro, you are out of your mind. Close to death and first thing you say… is can you still sing!" They fell out laughing.

But I was serious. *If I'd come out of surgery alive, and I couldn't sing…* Fortunately, your vocal chords are the strongest muscles you have if you keep using them. To this day I almost have the same natural tenor voice I had as a twenty-year-old. The surgery didn't affect my vocal chords at all. I was relieved that after I healed I could join my brothers performing again. I never believed for a minute that if they got sick, their health wouldn't bounce back like mine did.

Lawrence never told us that he went to see a neurologist at this time, or that his PSA level was high, an indicator of possible prostate cancer. It wasn't that he was keeping that information from us, he was in denial himself. He didn't go back for his regular check-up six months later like the doctor ordered. He tried to put it out of his mind for over a year. Meanwhile, we kept performing all over the country, a high energy, grueling schedule, even when you're in good shape.

We were working at the Tropicana Hotel in Atlantic City the next year, booked for the whole weekend. On Friday night Lawrence began telling us how bad he felt. He had this boil on his butt and wanted to find a doctor to lance it. We all felt that with a little rest, and being off his feet, he'd feel better the next day. Instead, when he awoke, the pain was so bad he apologized about not being able to do the show that night. We managed without him, scuffling through, apologizing to the audience, promising that Lawrence would be back again in no time. We had no idea how serious it was. By the next night it was apparent that we couldn't finish our Tropicana engagement. Still, we thought it was just a boil, maybe infected. Nothing to really worry about it.

Back home in Detroit, Lawrence saw his regular doctor who admitted him to the hospital. That's when we found out that he had cancer. By that time it had spread from his prostate to other parts of his body, including his liver. He was immediately transferred up to the University of Michigan for treatment. There was nothing the rest of us could do but keep working and praying. It felt horrible being so helpless. We were used to solving all our problems together, supporting each other through thick and thin. This was something we hadn't anticipated, especially at this stage of life. Lawrence was just fifty-nine years old. As a group, we were still very much in demand and counted on performing for many years to come.

By then the sad reality of losing Lawrence had started to sink in. The career high we should have felt when we learned in 1997 that The Four Tops were awarded a star on the Hollywood Walk of Fame didn't really register. We were thrilled that we had been chosen, especially since in those days, it was mostly actors and movie stars who were picked to represent the best in the Hollywood industry. We flew out to sunny L.A. The wonderful ceremony had a bittersweet element. Too sick to travel, the most musically gifted member of our group, our earliest music director and arranger, wasn't there to hear Berry Gordy extol us in such a heartfelt way: "These are four of the greatest people I have ever known. They were major pros even before they came to Motown." Our families and more than three hundred fans were in attendance to help us celebrate. Yet with all the people around, Lawrence was never far from our thoughts.

A month later I was in Atlanta, celebrating my daughter Farah's graduation from Spelman College. My joy overflowed

Obie, Levi and I unveil our star on the Hollywood Walk of Fame, 1997.
TSUNI USA/ALAMY

watching her receive her diploma among a sea of other beautiful young women I knew were bound for great things. I couldn't help but think of my other daughter Kai, who also attended Spelman years before, but dropped out. Since high school, she had concealed a drinking problem from her mother and me. I wish I had been able to save her from her downward spiral. Many American families have suffered the heartbreaking loss of a loved one with a drug or alcohol problem that they just can't kick. Looking back I can think of all the things I should have, could have done. If only you can go back and fix your mistakes. I guess I did the best I could until I was able to free myself from my own addiction so I could be a better father. Losing Kai made me hold onto Farah even tighter.

Farah is the best combination of Piper and me: beautiful, ambitious, and smart. She went on to become a lawyer like her mother. At her law school graduation, she introduced me to the exceptional young man she had fallen in love with and would eventually marry, Ralph Cook, a Morehouse man from Birmingham, Alabama. I'll never forget when Ralph called her mother and me a few years later to ask for Farah's hand in marriage. I was really impressed that he was man enough and mannerable enough to make the gesture. I asked him when he planned to pop the question. He told me that he wanted to take her to Paris to stay at her favorite hotel. Farah loved Paris and spoke French fluently, so he thought it would be the ideal place. I was impressed and gave him our blessing.

Later, I shared our conversation with Levi. "Guess what,

Lee, this guy is in love with Farah, and he wants to take her to Paris to propose."

Levi was as impressed as I was. "Is this boy white?" he asked. We cracked up. Of course, I would have welcomed any young man regardless of color into our family. All I can say is that Ralph Cook is a great young man, all the things a parent could hope for their daughter.

At Farah and Ralph's wedding reception, Levi and I sat together listening to Theo Peoples sing 'I Believe in You and Me.' We looked around savoring the breathtaking celebration that Piper put together (which I paid handsomely for). Levi smiled, taking it all in. "Man, this is outta sight, you really did it up."

"It's Farah," I told him. "If she hadn't picked a guy like Ralph, we wouldn't be here drinking champagne. We'd be at the Holiday Inn drinking beer."

They say for everything there is a time and season. Farah was born after my career was solidified. I didn't make some of the same mistakes I did with my first family. She is my pride and joy and has given me two amazing granddaughters, Carly and Riley. I also have another five wonderful grandchildren: Kai's children, Joy and Darren; and Nazim's kids, Yazim, Najma, and Allana. Having grandchildren later in my life and career has given me the time to spend with the next generation of my family. Being with them and my daughter Farah's in-laws has enriched my life so much. I now appreciate my time at home way more than being out on the road. But what lay ahead with Farah, Ralph, and their little family, all that happiness and joy, was yet to come as I sat in Spelman's Sisters Chapel, watching her walk across the dais to receive her diploma. That day in May 1997, my thoughts couldn't help but drift back to Lawrence, fighting for his life back in Detroit. I dreaded the feeling in the pit of my stomach that one day soon I'd be sitting in another church on a much more somber occasion.

During the next month, the Tops were hard at work performing on the road, trying to make do with just three members of the group in an act that required four voices. Whenever I was in town, I'd go to the hospital and give Lawrence his share of our earnings. It brightened his mood to see me, hear about what was happening with the group, but I could tell he wasn't feeling great. The cancer had spread to his bladder and other parts of his body. Finally, they said they'd done everything they could to try to control it, but it was too far gone. They sent him home. Even then, we made every effort to have little meetings with him, talking like we always did, but it became too difficult for him to speak. So we did most of the talking. He'd just nod. We kept it up, praying, hoping for some miracle. Lawrence was the youngest one of us and we weren't prepared to let him go. "Lord, take one of us," we prayed. "Let one of us take his place." But he just kept getting worse and after a couple of weeks, he knew, we knew, that it would be any day. And one day in June 1997 he just eased on out.

Even though we knew it was coming, it was the biggest shock, the biggest hurt we could have ever experienced. Like losing a limb, a brother, a real family member. We all had brothers we grew up with, but I think we felt stronger for each other than for our own blood brothers. Our grief brought us so low. We weren't sure we wanted to go on without him. Finally, Lawrence's son, Lawrence Jr., consoled us. He shared that his dad made his peace with his Father before he passed on. He gave Lawrence Jr. his ring, telling him to take care of things when he was gone.

Lawrence was given a big homegoing service at Oak Grove with people coming from all over the country—business people, family, friends, and fans. By the time BeBe Winans sang, tears were flowing freely. And when they closed Lawrence's casket, we walked down, reached out, and put our hands on top of it, touching him for the last time. We broke down, we couldn't help ourselves. We cried like babies. It was inconceivable that he was truly gone.

Lawrence was marvelous. He was a quiet man, with an inner strength and power that you didn't see coming. When he put his mind to something, he went about it with such intensity and stealth. My nickname for him was Quiet Storm. He didn't make a big deal about his musicianship, his singing, writing and arranging, but his talent was formidable, undeniable.

One day when we were very young, Lawrence's wife was mad at him about something. She came home really angry. She asked Lawrence Jr. where his father was. Junior pointed to a room where The Four Tops were rehearsing. She charged over, ready to fling the door open, and then she stopped. We were in the midst of singing a beautiful song, really pretty. She just stopped and listened. Junior said, "So you going in, Ma?"

"Naw," she said, not moving, "I just want to listen for a while." For a long time she just sat there. Then she walked away. She couldn't confront him because she felt too much, too much love, too much emotion, coming from that song. Junior told us it was one of the most beautiful sounds that he'd ever heard from a group. That's when we were young, singing those beautiful harmonies, with those young voices.

We sang a last song for him at the funeral, one that Lawrence had written a few years earlier, 'The Four of Us.'

Now there were only three of us, but that day singing, we tried to touch the sun…

The four of us
We put our expectations to the sky
And the only consolation was that we try
Laugh and cry, live and die
Kept our pride
We're still the four of us

Remember when we tried to touch the sun
I recall that on the way
We had such fun, with everyone
Every boy and girl, around the world knows
That there'll always be, through eternity
There'll always be
The four of us

We gave our God sent talent to the world
With unbending courage
We took the good and bad
Glad and sad
Rain or shine, for all time
We're still the four of us

Remember when we tried to touch the sun?
I recall that on the way
We had such fun
There'll always be
Through eternity
There'll always be…
The four of us…

In the days that followed Lawrence's funeral, we were lost. We talked about what we were going to do, business-wise. Should we just go ahead and quit? We'd always said if one of us wasn't there, none of us could be there. But somehow, after days of talking, hugging, and working through our grief, we decided to carry on. It was then that we decided that no matter what, we weren't going to put anyone in Lawrence's spot. Or change our name to The Three Tops or simply the Tops, which our agents and manager urged us to do. We held firm that we'd worked together for years to remain a foursome, which was our identity. The Four Tops was a brand not a number. No matter how much they bugged us, we stayed The Four Tops in name and spirit.

It took about a year or so before we started getting weary doing our show with just three voices. Sometimes we used one of our musicians, our conductor, to sing the fourth part. It gave us some ease vocally, but we still felt like there was something missing onstage. After a while, Levi and I got to talking about the need for another guy. No one could ever fill Lawrence's shoes but maybe they could fill the empty space.

The Temptations had just released a singer, Theo Peoples, the baritone who had replaced Richard Street, originally the Paul Williams spot back in the day. The Temptations had cycled through a number of replacements for the original members. We felt Theo would be a good fit for a Top; he was a great group singer and could sing harmonies and lead too. I could tell that Levi was getting tired, and I had to confess, I was too. Lawrence's passing was like a wake-up call. We needed to take better care of our bodies, not push our limits.

We decided to reach out to Theo about joining us to sing background, and lead now and then to give Levi a break. Personally, I'd always felt that Theo sounded too much like a Temptation. He had a loud, slick quality to his delivery, not smooth and mellow like a Top, but he was good enough to fill in. After Theo joined, we had a few good years of performing to sold out crowds who loved the show and embraced the change in our line-up. We were working hard to give them the same sound and showmanship, but the inevitable eventually closed in.

It was at an outdoor amphitheater in North Carolina, where we were booked for three nights with The Beach Boys, that Levi couldn't go on. His legs were weak and his voice was straining. Prior to our performance that afternoon, he called me to his room, sounding really bad. "Duke, I can't go on. I can't take another step. I can't sing another note. Sorry, man, I just can't do it."

"Man, you're kidding me," I said, realizing he wasn't at his best, but we'd always managed to muster enough energy to go on with the show. Plus I wasn't ready to go down this route… not with Levi.

"I'm tired," he said, flat out, no motivation, nothing.

"You've been saying that for the last couple of years," I had to admit. "But we gotta do this weekend man, we got a sold-out house." I was hoping to get through this engagement, then he could take a rest and bounce back like he always did.

"Duke, I'm sorry, do whatever you got to do," he said, as he started packing his bags to go home.

With a heavy heart, like it or not, I knew it was time to give Theo the football. I told Levi what the plan was, and he agreed. When we first hired Theo, we'd instructed him to learn the words and lyrics to the songs in case he'd be called upon to fill in for Levi one day.

When I went to Theo's room to let him know he was taking over for Levi that night, he took a minute. "Duke, let me say, I know the songs, but I cannot remember all them mother fucking words to all them songs."

He could tell from my reaction that this wasn't the right answer.

"I've been practicing, but I can't remember," he pleaded.

"Damn, we better think of something," I said, pacing, trying to figure out how to move forward.

"Oh shit, I got it!" Theo said jumping up, an idea occurring to him. "I'm going to my computer, get all the lyrics to the songs and I'm going to print them out in a big font. Paste the songs across the floor onstage with all those lyrics."

"That's a brilliant idea," I said. "You think it can work?"

"Yeah, I think I can do that," Theo said, taking out his computer.

With that solved, Theo replacing Levi, we still needed another voice. Ronnie McNeir, who we'd hired as a back-up for our piano player, could also sing. We had also instructed him to prepare vocals in case we needed him one day. That day had come. "Ronnie," I said to him, "you're going to have to be a Top, starting tonight."

He was reluctant, but I reassured him.

"Man, you know enough of these songs. You can fake it for now, you're just going to have to do it for tonight."

As showtime approached, Theo was still working on his lyrics, and the rest of us were in the dressing room getting ready to go on. Ronnie complained that we didn't have a pair of matching shoes big enough to fit his feet. By that point it didn't matter to me what color his shoes were. I told him to wear a pair of his own shoes. They weren't like ours, but we had no other choice.

Ronnie wasn't going for it. "I'm not wearing shoes that don't match. You got to find me some."

"People ain't going to pay no attention to that shit, man. Just get up there and sing." He had his doubts, and I knew his stage fright would be lessened if he had confidence in the way he looked. But I figured we'd just plough through it.

But the minute we went onstage, opening with the beautiful ballad 'MacArthur Park', someone in the audience screamed, "Wait a minute, where's Levi!?" Then another voice taunted, "Hey man, what's up with them shoes!?" Ronnie looked at me and his look said everything, "*I told you.*" But we got through that show and every other show that weekend. For a while that was the Tops' line-up. Eventually, Levi retired and we made it official. However, he did make one auspicious come back.

In the winter of 1999, President Clinton invited us to perform at a holiday party as he was leaving office after his second term. We considered him a friend, having performed at the Arkansas Governor's mansion in the beginning of his political career. Twice when he was President, we sang at his birthday celebrations at the White House. He told us that we were his favorite Motown act, and he even accompanied us on his saxophone one time. When Levi heard that Clinton wanted us to perform again, he said, "Duke, let's make this motherfucker happy."

It made *me* happy that Levi felt good enough to sing. "Think you can make it?" I asked hopefully.

"I'm going to make it, man," he said. "I'm not going to miss this."

And what better place to perform your last show than at the White House?

* * *

Now Obie and I were the last of the Tops still performing. I kept reminding myself that half of four was better than nothing. But I had to admit that I was slowing up too. In the beginning of our career when we were just getting it together, I used to do a whole lot for the group. I was the manager, road manager, valet, everything. I would take the clothes to the cleaners, store them in my house in the basement. When we had engagements, I'd get them out, take them to the dressing room where we all got dressed together. I laid our wardrobe out like a real valet. I'd help everyone pull it together. I was the one who talked to the agencies, booked all of our engagements, coordinated schedules for transportation, musicians, payroll, everything. Even when I was drinking, I handled it. Obie would laughingly say, "Motherfucker, you can do more shit in a day drunk then most motherfuckers can do in a week sober."

Now my instincts told me that I should start looking for another replacement in case something happened to either one of us. The scrambling I did the night that Theo taped his lyrics to the floor and Ronnie wore brown shoes wasn't going to happen again. Especially with me being a stickler for the level of polish and professionalism the Tops were known for. I thought I had a little time to put the word out, scout singers, listen to new talent. Then Obie stubbed his toe real bad—at least, that's what we thought it was. After about a week, it started to go black and the pain shot up his leg. He complained to me that he could barely keep up the pace onstage, so we brought in doctors, physical therapists, and masseuses to rub his legs and keep him moving. When we got home, the doctor told him that he had gangrene. "That's bullshit," Obie told the man and left his office.

Obie was the most happy-go-lucky guy you'd ever want to meet. When he was young, he had a velvety smooth baritone bass that sounded just like Nat King Cole. He had a winning smile to match. Everyone loved him. But as wonderful as he could be, he could turn on you. Every now and then when Obie drank another side of him would come out, and you didn't want to be around him. But for the most part, Obie was just so much fun to be around; his personality was irresistible.

I could always count on him with challenging business situations that took teamwork to fix. If I had to talk with someone I didn't really know that well, or I wasn't sure how to get to through to them, I'd introduce them to Obie. He'd just start talking with the wonderful way he had with people. With his great smile and infectious personality, folks would just open up to him. He would take them to the bar, have a drink, sit down for a meal, telling jokes and getting them as loose as a goose. Then he'd come to me and say, "Duke, he's ready."

The four of us always put the group first. It was the way we looked at things. Like when we got our first apartment in New York (the time we took over the mic at Birdland), we had just enough money to pay the first month's rent. We had to figure out what do about the next month. The older lady who managed the building liked us. We enjoyed hanging around her and her kids, talking about show business, eating dinner. We began to notice she was developing a soft spot for Obie, always smiling, quite fond of him.

Eventually, rent time came around and we hadn't made a dime. Obie volunteered to go up to the lady's apartment to discuss our predicament with her. He took a bottle of Old Granddad with him. When he returned, he breathed a sigh of relief, saying we didn't have to worry, it was taken care of. With his winning ways, Obie was usually able to talk his way out of anything.

This went on for about six more months while we were struggling to pay the bills. Every month Obie would grab his bottle of Old Granddad and go upstairs. Finally, we were able to start working enough to regularly pay the rent in cash. But Obie helped us get through a tough time with his warmth and affability. She wasn't the owner of the building, maybe she was part-owner, and we never knew if she paid our rent herself or what the deal was. But she really helped us out at a crucial time, even introducing us to an important manager who booked some gigs for us in the Catskills. He also managed a fabulous tap-dancing act called Hines and Sons: a young Gregory Hines and his older brother, Maurice, and their father. We got to know them really well.

Obie was a great dancer, too, and helped put together the choreography for the group. The Tops were known for our "crisp moves," very suave and smooth, which was the style that evolved after Billy Eckstine got on us for trying too hard. When Theo Peoples took Lawrence's spot, it was Obie who taught him our dance routine. That was one of his fortes. So what happened next must have really come as a shock to him.

While the Tops were performing at a big Christmas party for

a prominent Detroit attorney, Geoffrey Fieger, Obie passed out in the middle of the show. A few weeks later, Obie complained about pain in his toe and leg. A doctor examined him, but he never revealed what his condition was. Obie returned to work but soon the pain became too excruciating. Obie was admitted to a hospital, and this doctor confirmed his diagnosis: he had gangrene and might have to have his leg removed from below the knee. After pitching a fit, ranting and raving, the surgery was performed. As soon as Obie came to, he wanted to get up and out. "Obie, you don't have no leg, man," someone broke it to him.

High on morphine and painkillers, he really lost his mind, cursing the doctor out: "Motherfucker, I came to you with a hurt leg and a bad toe and you cut off my whole motherfucking leg!" He called me to come down to the hospital and get him out. Hoping, as a team, the two of us could fix it. I rushed down, desperate to put his mind at ease, to try to talk some sense to him. I explained that after he recuperated, they were going to fit him for a nice prosthetic leg. In time, he'd be back on his feet again. He didn't want to hear any of it. All he wanted was out. Instead, they kept him to do more testing. Finally, they discovered that he had stage four-lung cancer. He had been a heavy smoker.

Obie made the decision to have no more operations, whatever happened. "Just get me out of here," he told his daughter, Tobi. I'd known that Obie's condition was bad. But I had no idea just how bad. A few days after his leg was amputated, I was at breakfast and I got a phone call: "Come to the hospital. Obie just passed away." I jumped up in shock. Crying, I rushed over, and sure enough he was gone. It happened that fast.

With Obie gone, I was faced with the difficult agenda of reinventing the Tops. Not knowing Obie's absence would be permanent, Lawrence Jr. had been temporarily singing in his spot since he was admitted to hospital. We never expected this would last for long, but Junior was very talented. Just like his father, he had a good musical ear, and he knew all the band's arrangements and the steps to our routines. He was a great little dancer. Now was also the time to give Theo Peoples his departing letter. I explained, like I had since the beginning, that he sounded too much like a Temptation. I'd been urging him all along to try to sing more naturally. His reply was always, "I can't do it no better than this." I guess he really was doing his best. Still, I brought in Harold "Spike" Bonhart to sing Levi's part. Spike had a strong voice, a very soulful, straight-pop kind of voice. He could throw in a little harsh, raw quality when needed. Even so, no one could ever replicate Levi's voice. But this line-up kept the group going, especially during the difficult transition period when all I wanted to do was grieve my sick and departed brothers.

Losing Lawrence and Obie devastated me but having Levi still alive was my greatest consolation. He wasn't by my side every night singing, but I could still call or drop by his house to talk to him whenever I wanted. Levi was the only Top who stayed married to the same woman his whole life, Clineice. From the time they courted back in Idlewild, the young dancer and the young singer were devoted to each other. She took such good care of him after he had a stroke and was bedridden. It was hard to see my partner like that, the man who was once so handsome, witty, and debonair.

When Levi walked into a room people gravitated to him. He had true charisma, that quality they call the "it" factor. Onstage his presence was electrifying. I'd witnessed it before I met him, the first time I saw him singing as a young boy at the Paradise Theater talent show. Levi knew that he had been blessed with a God-given talent, but he didn't take it for granted. He worked hard. Singing back-up at Motown, waiting for a hit record to break, gave the Tops time to learn how to be recording artists. That was when Levi learned how to project that magnificent voice of his, convey his feelings through a microphone. He already knew how to do that onstage, but it's a totally different thing when you're recording. Onstage you have the audience giving you energy, so you can exchange what's inside you back to them. In the studio, all you have is a microphone, the music, and you. You have to find that inner spirit, your inner soul to put out vocally. Levi had the ability to convey really deep, powerful emotions in the studio. His voice was strong and forceful, but it also had a cry to it, a masculine, robust, crying feeling. That's why his voice caught on so well with the women. He had that plea. It was as close to the sound of love as a singer can convey and closer to salvation. It had a holiness to it.

When Levi passed in 2008, I thought I had been hit hard before, but this time it crushed me. Nothing could have prepared me. He'd had a series of strokes, and it was difficult for him to even talk. Still, I'd sit with him and have conversations. Me doing all the chatting, him trying to communicate. I couldn't understand a word of what he was saying. In the end, he suffered from high blood pressure and diabetes, and his teeth were totally deteriorated dating back from the time a dentist in England had messed up. He was miserable, lying in one spot, moaning and groaning. His passing was merciful for him, but it just killed me.

With Levi gone it was the first time in my life that I felt truly alone. I had a wonderful family, but a part of my life was now over. Not only was Levi my first connection with The Four Tops, he was also my last. My whole adult life, Levi had always been a shoulder to lean on. The someone I turned for advice or consolation. The group always had consultations about decisions that affected us. If one of my buddies said he didn't like something, if one of our voices was undecided, we'd just keep talking until we all came to an agreement. Not until we all could say right or wrong, live or die, did we make a decision. Whatever that decision was, we were all behind it one hundred per cent. And now those voices were silent. It wasn't that I was afraid to be alone. I just wasn't used to it. It had been so many years. Decades.

The night before Levi's funeral, I had another one of my dreams. My three buddies Obie, Levi, and Lawrence, came to me. "Duke, before you go, remember what we used to talk about? Many times. How wonderful our life has been, how people have treated us so well, especially in the early years? Whatever you do, don't forget to tell them thank you. It all went by so fast. We didn't have a chance to say goodbye. Or thank you. Tell them for us. Tell them thank you."

And that's what I did. At Levi's funeral, I looked out at all the people who were so full of grief, and I said, "You may not believe this, but my buddies came to me last night. They told me to tell you this before I go… how grateful they are. Each one of you who helped us along our way. When we were young and poor you loaned us cab fares, took us to our engagements when we didn't have a ride. Mothers out there who fed us when we were hungry. One guy blew out his car engine taking us to a gig in Carolina. He didn't say nothing about it, just dropped us off. I don't know how he got home, but he helped us make our gig. People like Arthur Braggs up in Idlewild, who bought us our first car when were just kids. It had a record player in, it was amazing. If we were hungry the four of us would drive that car up to Idlewild and spend the weekend with him and his wife. She'd cook us all kinds of food. We had a bedroom to sleep in, and we just ate and rested and dreamed. The buddy that loaned me five dollars to get our uniforms out the dry cleaners. The people that bought our first records. The ones who bought tickets to our concerts. The ones who mentioned our names to everyone they knew to help us get started. You all helped make The Four Tops. Obie, Levi, and Lawrence say thank you, thank you, thank you, thank you. Especially Levi, thank you for the wonderful life and the wonderful ride you've given us."

I left the stage in tears. Lawrence Jr. and I had planned to sing 'The Four of Us' with the new members of the group. I just couldn't do it. I don't know why, but I didn't want to sing that song then. I was all by myself with only the memories. Great memories of my buddies and the things that we accomplished. The love we spread.

From then on, I took it upon myself to do what I thought the three of them would want me to. The way The Four Tops would have done it. That's the only way.

❧ 11 ❧

The Uncharted Road

Family, legacy, and the future of The Four Tops are my main focus since the road behind me stretches longer than the road ahead. There was a time when I thought that my son, Abdul Jr., "Dula," would follow in my footsteps, the perfect replacement. He looks like me, same height, about the same weight, but he can't sing a note. Dula handles the technical part of our show, setting up the sound system. He makes it possible for the Tops to move to dozens of different venues with different acoustics and challenges and have our voices sound as good as our recordings. Performing away from home so much, I love having my son with me. The band tells me that he sings my part as he sets everything up for us. That he keeps getting better. I hope that I live to see the day.

At the end of 2008, soon after Levi passed, I started having some professional regrets, and with all of the guys gone I reached out to Dula. It was around Christmas time and I was feeling kind of blue. I confided that with all the wonderful records The Four Tops made, I was disappointed that we'd never won a Grammy. One great song or another had always beaten us out, which was okay then. There was always tomorrow. Now in the evening of my career I didn't see a chance of ever getting one.

"We achieved every one of the things we aspired to do in the business," I told him. "It's the one thing that slipped away from us."

"Don't worry about it, Dad," Dula reassured me. "Your career has been monumental. People have adored you all these years. You've been inducted in the Rock and Roll Hall of Fame. You have a star on the Hollywood Walk of Fame. *Rolling Stone* named you in the 100 Greatest Artists of all time. Don't let it bug you."

Two days later the phone rang.

"Duke Fakir?"

"Yes."

"This is Neil Portnow, President of the Recording Academy. You've just been selected for the Academy's highest honor: a Grammy Lifetime Achievement Award."

Tears started rolling down my face. It was the little hole that was missing. Not that I wasn't grateful for what we already had.

"You really mean it?" I said.

"Yes, I'll send you the information about coming to Hollywood for the show."

I hung up and immediately called Dula. "You are not going to believe this," I said, barely believing it myself, "I just got a Grammy." He dropped the phone, jumping for joy.

Dula was by my side in L.A. along with Piper, Farah and Ralph, and other family members at the award ceremony on the Saturday. Johnny Mathis and other artists we'd admired along the way were also in attendance. I was the last one to speak and thanked everybody. "Having a Grammy for a hit record or two would have been great, but the Lifetime Achievement Award means so much more. It covers many Grammys. A lifetime of doing the best you can for as long as you can. And it's your peers

With my daughter Farah and my Lifetime Achievement Grammy, 2009.

who anoint you with this honor. For me it's one of the greatest honors I have ever received. Thank you. And thank you on behalf of The Four Tops who no are longer here who share this honor with me." The highlight of the televised award show the next night was Jamie Foxx, Smokey Robinson, and Neo, three of the most celebrated singers in the industry, singing Obie, Lawrence, and Levi's parts. We performed a medley of Four Tops classic tunes, 'Reach Out I'll Be There,' 'Standing in the Shadows of Love', and 'I Can't Help Myself.'

Just before we went onstage, I looked in the mirror with my Grammy in hand and tried to summon my three partners. "Obie, Levi, Lawrence, I just wish you were here. This is just as much yours as it is mine. Thank you, guys. I love you, God bless you." Then I went onstage and sang my heart out. I looked out at the front row and there was my old friend, Paul McCartney, leading the audience jumping to their feet, applauding. An amazing night, one that I shall always cherish.

Getting a Grammy like that, after putting it out in the universe and two days later it manifesting, reinforced my belief that someone, some power greater than me, really is out there listening. It was another message from above, helping me answer the question most of us share about the meaning of life… *is there a bigger reason?* The Four Tops' success wasn't simply about personal desire; there was a higher purpose than just us singing, larger than each of us individually. What the group represented—brotherhood, loyalty, and people connecting and loving each other—was that the reason that destiny played the winning hand? We were put on earth to help spread a message in the universal language that everyone understands, man, woman, child, regardless of color, nationality, ethnicity, sexual orientation… music. After receiving that epiphany, my efforts to keep The Four Tops alive were renewed.

Lawrence Jr.'s father "passed the baton" on to him for the future generation. I'm just trying to pass on the knowledge. When he first joined the group, he posed an interesting question. "Duke, do you think one of the original members of the group would have kept the Tops going if you were gone?"

"You really want me to be honest?" I asked him. I could tell he wanted to hear the truth, so I told him how years ago I tried an experiment. I told the guys that for one week, once a month, each one of them should take over running the organization from top to bottom, in order to see what really went into it. From paying people, to making sure all the invoices were paid, handling the finances etc. They all agreed.

Lawrence Sr. said up front, "I really don't want to be a part of it, but okay, man, if the rest of y'all are going to do it, I'll go along with it."

The first one up was Levi. We had a weekend engagement. He made sure that the payroll was taken care of on the road. We were paid half of it. The other half had been sent to our office as a deposit before we left. So Levi paid everybody half and let them know that when we got home, "I'll take care of y'all there too." Well, when we got back home we called Levi for four days to get our money until we finally reached him.

"I forgot all about that shit, man," he said. "It was the furthest thing from my mind. Taking care of paying folks, fuck it, I can't do this shit. Why don't you come get this money and take care of it, Duke?" We all laughed. That was Levi.

Next up was Obie, I let him know it was his turn. He looked at me and said, "Duke, I don't feel like I want to pay nobody a fucking dime. That's the furthest thing from my mind, that's your job. I didn't like the idea going in, but I had to go along with everybody."

So I went to Lawrence. Lawrence started laughing, "Don't even come to me with that shit. Duke, you know that ain't me.

I give you all the songs. All the notes to sing. Just give me mine when it's time. That's all. You're doing a fine job with all that."

"Thanks," I said, "but y'all should know the business part too."

"We know," they said, "ain't nobody complaining."

So we kept up doing what we always had, dividing it up four ways, with me handling all our business.

Hearing that story about the other Tops, the way he knew them, satisfied Lawrence Jr.'s curiosity. They loved the music, just not the business. Without my hand in things like money matters, someone else could have done the job, but not with the same commitment or the passion, and with the risk of them helping themself to the fruits of our labor. We were well aware of those nightmares. Some instances were too close to home to mention. I don't take all the credit. There were many ingredients to our career. Each one of us played key roles in our own ways. Our personalities meshed like our voices did. The truth is that none of us could have made it without the others. But no one else wanted to be bothered with the nuts-and-bolts things that I enjoyed. It went back to the days when I followed Daddy Braggs around, watching him click his counter when folks came in the club door, or even further back to my glee in taking inventory of the newspapers I collected for the war effort in elementary school. It was my privilege, my joy, to make sure that the Tops were on top of their business. It is still my pleasure to make sure that what we worked so hard to achieve keeps on going.

From time to time, I still feel a tinge of survivor's guilt that

I'm the one who's still alive. My brothers are gone. I used to think that there was no good reason that I should have outlived them, to be in the kind of health that I'm in, and be here to tell the story. For all the shit that I've been through, all the things that I've done (the same things as my partners) I always came out smelling like a rose. When I step back, with the insight I've gained from living long enough to see all the pieces and how they fit together, the bigger picture has begun to reveal itself. But some things still remain a wonderful mystery, like how I've always felt protected throughout my life. *But why me?*

I always go back to one thing. I started in the church. I was brought back to that same church. Church always had such great meaning for me. I knew it would help me put my life back on course. I tried to share that with my partners. "Guess what, man? You know we've talked about how the Lord has been with us all this time. He's given us everything under the sun you can imagine, family, joy, happiness, money, success. I think He wants us to pay Him back. I think He wants His glory."

Levi heard me and came to church with me one time. He left before the service was over. Later, he apologized for walking out, but I let him know I didn't judge him. Somewhere in the back of my mind, I kept wondering if the reason I'm still here and they're gone is because they didn't give *HIM* the praise *HE* deserves. When you're young you think, "*We worked hard for this, we earned it,*" but it's not all about you. You have to make that connection. Eventually, I think Lawrence did. Near the end, when he found out that he had cancer and was bedridden, I think he made his peace with God. We all go through learning and changing at different times. I know all the Tops believed in God. That's good enough. It could just have been their time to go. They each had done their thing, and the Lord said, "Time for you to come home. You raised your families well. Made good. You kept your word, the promise you made." We each have to do it our own way.

One of the numbers that we perform truly captures the spirit of our story. Frank Sinatra's wistful ballad 'My Way' is a part of The Four Tops' standard repertoire. About four years ago, I realized that the way Frank Sinatra sang it was perfect for him, but the truth of the Tops was something quite different. So I changed a few lyrics and now I sing the solo part. I tell the audience when I introduce the song about the first time we sang together at Joanne Artist's graduation party when we were teens. How out of all the people Levi and I knew, we just happened to pick Lawrence and Obie. The moment we sang together, out came such magical sounds. From then on, we knew that it really wasn't our way, it was *God's way*. Sure we worked hard, but it took more than us. It took the hand of God, who turned things our way. Performing our version of 'My Way' in venues all over the country, I never thought I could sing a solo every night and always get a standing ovation. People come up to me afterwards and say, "Thank you, Duke, you brought tears to my eyes." It makes me so proud.

Singing with a new group of talented guys has been a blessing. Ronnie McNeir, Lawrence "Roquel" Payton Jr., and Alex Morris are the new line-up. They're as close to the original Tops as you can get. But I have to school the guys that there's more to being a Top than just singing. To be a Top you have to act like a Top. I have to give them a little history, explain how we conducted ourselves, the way we approached our jobs. "Don't think of this as just as a paying engagement. People love us. You have to treat them the same way, treat them beautifully. When people ask for autographs give it to them gladly. These are people who paid to see you. When they want to see you after the show gladly give your time. Onstage don't just go up there and sing the song. Sing to the people, look them in the eye, and make contact with them. Let them share what you're feeling."

I hear myself channeling my mentor, Billy Eckstine, who shared his knowledge with me when I was a young and aspiring upstart. "You've got to love the audience. If you win them over they're yours. That's who will carry you on to bigger heights, but it's gotta come from your heart. You have to be loyal to them and they will be loyal to you."

How you treat the fans is a simple thing to convey. How to perform like a Top takes work and comes from years of experience. The first thing you need to know is how to get on and off the stage. If you walk out on the stage looking fabulous and your audience says, "Wow, look at them!" you shock them and make them feel good. That's number one. A big-time singer once tried to tell me, "Naw, when you hit the stage, it's all about the singing." We enjoyed the ensuing argument. Neither of us changed our minds. What I know is that the minute you hit the stage, before you even open your fucking mouth, you have to look like something. If people like what they see, you're one step ahead.

Second thing is when you do open your mouth, you sing something that's going to get to them. One of their favorite hits or something that they love. Then at the end when you leave the stage, they should be happy, singing, jumping up and down. They should be as happy as a fat boy eating cake. That's show business. All show business is built on that. If you want to know what to do in the middle, do something that touches their heart. Our middle number is one that they'll remember.

I'm still the one who puts the show together. The one who designs the clothes, sets the order of the show, paces it. If we're in the middle of a number, and it's not flowing, I'll switch it up. I'll tell the conductor before he goes to the intro of the next song, "Hold it, hold it right there…" I talk a lot between the songs and the audience likes it. They like a little history. They want to be a part of it. I say, "Hold it, nephew…" because my nephew is the conductor. Then I tell the audience, "My heart tells me to do this song. I don't know whether you want to hear it, but here it comes." They love it. I do have a little knowledge about the stage because I feel it; it's not something I do on autopilot. I've been doing it for almost sixty-five years, but every night before the show, I'm anxious, not excited, just anxious to get out there and see what the audience has to give me.

People ask me if I ever get tired singing our hit records? I say, "fuck naw." Every night's a different audience, every night it's a different love, a different respect. I look in people's eyes, and as long as I see that respect, that enjoyment, that thank you, I'll sing that motherfucker till the day I die.

Recently, in Pennsylvania, I fell and injured my hip pretty badly. It hurt like hell, but we were en route to another show in New Jersey. So I got on that bus, made the three-hundred-mile trip and performed that night in a wheelchair. A little pain never stopped me. I really wasn't aware of the extent of my injury, for me the show must go on. When I got back to Detroit, a frantic Piper drove me directly to the hospital. The break I sustained was serious enough for me to have another hip replacement, having had my first in 2002. Less than a month later, I was back performing again, only missing one scheduled show. I had the stage manager wheel me onstage, and I made an announcement to the audience before they saw me, explaining what happened and that I was going to be performing sitting down. Off the top of my head I said, "I'm not gonna be hippin' or hoppin', dancing or prancing, I'll just be singing and swinging." Then the lights came up and I was sitting there, dressed to the nines. They saw that I was still there for them, and they loved it. They gave me a standing ovation before and after the show.

At this stage in my career, I take it all in stride, the highs and lows. I've been going since 1954, and the journey hasn't been always been smooth. We've definitely had a few bumps in the road, but when asked about the pitfalls, it's hard to even remember them. The highs are what shine through. The only pitfall I see is that the three of them are not here with me.

I know the best thing I do in life is singing. I'm not going to ever retire, the Lord can retire me, but I'm not going into the dark night quietly. I know I'm not in the fourth quarter anymore, I'm in overtime. And the day I hear my last applause, lights out, final curtain, I hope I hear those three magical voices blending in with mine…

Now if you feel that you can't go on
Because all of your hope is gone…
And you feel the world has grown cold
And you're drifting out all on your own
And you need a hand to hold…
Reach out
Reach out, reach out for me
I'll be there, with a love that will comfort you
And I'll be there, to cherish and care for you
I'll be there…

It's been a long time. Too long without the sound of those other voices. But I've loved every minute. And I am still enjoying the hell out of it.

Acknowledgements

I am deeply indebted to many important people in my life, too numerous to mention by name. The many good friends who have helped me along my path to success and stood by me through hard times as well. My professional colleagues who have consistently given me encouragement, and a helping hand along the way. My loving family, who've believed in me since the beginning, and now include a wonderful new generation of children and grandchildren. My dear friend and co-author, Kathleen McGhee-Anderson, whose talent and vision helped me to tell my story and is like family. And finally, to my dear departed brothers, Levi, Obie, and Lawrence, they're with me every step I take, every note I sing.

Permissions

'Reach Out I'll Be There'
Words and Music by Lamont Dozier, Brian Holland and
Edward Jr. Holland
© 1966
Reproduced by permission of Stone Agate Music, London
W1F 9LD.

'The Four of Us'
Words and Music by Lawrence Payton
©1987
Reproduced by permission of Oval Music and Stone
Diamond Music corp, London W1F 9LD.

'MacArthur Park'
Words and Music by Jimmy Webb
© 1968 Universal – Polygram International Publishing, Inc.
Copyright renewed
All rights reserved. Used by permission of Hal Leonard
Europe Ltd.